TRAINING THE TRANSLATOR

PAUL KUSSMAUL
Johannes-Gutenberg Universität Mainz

JOHN BENJAMINS PUBLISHING COMPANY
AMSTERDAM/PHILADELPHIA

The paper used in this publication meets the minimum requirements of American National Standard for Information Sciences — Permanence of Paper for Printed Library Materials, ANSI Z39.48-1984.

Library of Congress Cataloging-in-Publication Data

Kussmaul, Paul.
  Training the translator / Paul Kussmaul.
     p.   cm. -- (Benjamins translation library, ISSN 0929-7316 ; v. 10)
  Includes bibliographical references and indexes.
     1. Translators--Training of. 2. Translating and interpreting--Study and teaching. I. Title.
II. Series.
P306.5.K87   1995
418'.02'092--dc20   95-5027
ISBN 90 272 1609 6 (Eur.) / 1-55619-690-3 (US) (Hb; alk. paper)   CIP
ISBN 90 272 1623 1 (Eur.) / 1-55619-704-7 (US) (Pb; alk. paper)

John Benjamins Publishing Co. • P.O.Box 75577 • 1070 AN Amsterdam • The Netherlands
John Benjamins North America • P.O.Box 27519 • Philadelphia PA 191180-0519 • USA

Acknowledgements

This book grew out of my teaching in translator training courses at the Department of Applied Linguistics in Germersheim, University of Mainz (Germany) and also at universities in other parts of the world. I am indebted to my students who first of all made me see the problems that exist in translator training and who then helped me to shape my ideas by their valuable contributions in seminars and translation classes. A special word of gratitude goes to Mary Snell-Hornby who encouraged me to write this book. I am also grateful to several colleagues who read parts of the manuscript and made many valuable comments: to Hans and Sylvia Hönig and Don Kiraly of Mainz/Germersheim, to Frank G. Königs of Bochum, to Hans P. Krings of Hildesheim, to Wolfgang Lörscher of Leipzig, to Hans J. Vermeer of Heidelberg, to Wolfram Wilss of Saarbrücken, and to Rodney Sampson of Bristol who generously undertook the task of reading the entire manuscript. Finally I would like to thank Bertie Kaal of Benjamins Publishing Company for her cooperation and support during the final production stage. Needless to say, I alone am responsible for any remaining inadequacies.

To Gertrud

Contents

Introduction

On 30 June 1993, a round table discussion took place at the Department of Applied Linguistics in Germersheim, University of Mainz (Germany) at which translators and interpreters are trained. The subject of the discussion was the state of the market for professional translators. Among the issues raised were the nature and range of qualifications which a translator needed in order to cope with the tasks awaiting him. The participants, all of them professional translators, agreed that translators should be well-informed about special fields such as car-manufacturing, computer technology, and the law, and experts in the associated terminology. Also, they should have a near native-speaker competence in two, possibly three, foreign languages. Interestingly, at one point in the discussion, the chairman of a regional translators' association got up and maintained that a knowledge of linguistics and translation theory was in fact completely useless and would not help translators at all in their everyday work.

In a way, the last statement is typical of many people in the profession, and indeed of quite a number of teachers of translation. At the root of it is the idea that an engineer, lawyer or businessman/woman with a reasonable knowledge of foreign languages and a few good dictionaries at his or her disposal will be able to translate. What these people fail to see is that there is a distinction between factual knowledge and procedural knowledge, a distinction which was first brought to our notice some time ago by Wolfram Wilss, and more recently in Wilss 1993. Factual knowledge, i.e. knowledge of special fields, special terminology and foreign languages, is undoubtedly an essential requirement for translators. But it is not enough. We often come across texts involving experts sharing the same language which are hard to understand, even by other experts, because these texts lack for instance a coherent logical structure or fail to rouse and hold the reader's interest. The people who produced these texts knew what they were writing about, but they did not sufficiently know how to write. In the same way, translators must know *how* to translate. Translation, to put it briefly, is not just an exchange of words and structures, but a communicative process that takes into consideration the reader of the translation within a particular situation within a specific culture. People engaged in translation studies are trying to describe just how this process works.

Fortunately translation studies are not always faced with misunderstanding and opposition. There seems to be a growing awareness all over the world that we need methods for training translators, and that these methods should be concerned with the actual process of translation. Scholars of translation studies have been asked to talk about their methods not only in translator training institutions of Western and Eastern Europe and the Western World, but also in Middle Eastern Countries, India, China, Hong Kong, Indonesia, Thailand, South America and Africa. Translations have always been produced in these countries but it is now felt that the training of translators should be institutionalised and given a sound methodological basis.

Another sign of a positive attitude toward translation studies and of a growing awareness of the importance of the subject for translator training is the foundation of The European Society for Translation Studies (EST) in Vienna in 1992, which among other things, as stated in its constitution, offers consulting services on topics involving translation and interpreting and the teaching and training of these skills.

The present book fits in with this newer, method-oriented tradition. Accordingly, I shall not be concerned with the presentation of straightforward factual knowledge, nor shall I discuss how best to teach a foreign language, or specialised subject-areas or cultural studies. Furthermore, no attempt will be made to consider what details should be taught in these fields, although the proper selection of detailed knowledge is an important topic in translator training, and some improvements could certainly be made in this area. Instead, in this work the aim will be to explore various aspects of the methodology of translation.

It has been said that translation studies are not just concerned with matters of language alone but represent an interdisciplinary field, a view which for instance became apparent in the title of a congress in Vienna on September 9-12, 1992 *Translation Studies - An Interdiscipline* (Snell-Hornby et al. 1994). Certainly, in order to train specialists in technology, law, economics and medicine not only does the terminology of these disciplines have to be taught but also to some extent their scientific methods. To this end, we must look outside the confines of language in translator and interpreter training. Also, for the actual investigation of the translation process we cannot restrict ourselves to linguistics alone. The investigation of comprehension and production processes involves not only linguistic but also psychological, at least psycholinguistic and possibly also neurophysiological, knowledge and methods. Translating literary texts involves literary studies, and investigating creativity in translation involves the findings of creativity research.

It seems that the translation process is such a vast topic that one may feel discouraged even to begin looking at it. I shall therefore restrict myself for economy's sake. My approach still draws predominantly on linguistics, more specifically on psycholinguistics and textlinguistics. Within psycholinguistics I make use of such notions as bottom-up and top-down processing, activation of semantic features, prototypes, and scenes and frames. The notion of text linguistics favoured in this book includes the pragmatic dimension, that is to say the relation of the text to the author and to the reader of the text. Special emphasis is laid on the methods and models of descriptive stylistics, speech act theory, text-typology and functional sentence perspective. When talking about creativity in the second Chapter I shall include some of the basic concepts that have been developed by creativity research.

In the first Chapter, I begin by looking at the problems that students have when translating. In doing this, use is made of certain empirical methods which have been developed. Error Analysis and Think-aloud protocols are discussed and some findings made by myself and others on students' approaches are presented. Since no large-scale investigations have been carried out so far, these findings are still rather inconclusive. Nevertheless, it does not seem unreasonable to me to use them as a starting point for suggesting ways of helping our students to overcome the difficulties they have when they translate. Moreover, the presentation of the think-aloud-protocol-approach may stimulate teachers of translation who read this book to try this method with their own students. In the first Chapter the book may look somewhat error-biased and schoolmasterly. In order to counterbalance this impression, the second Chapter looks at successful translation processes observed in students, and specifically where processes involving creativity are concerned.

Ways to help our students form the topic of the following chapters. I begin with the most comprehensive frame of reference, pragmatic analysis (Chapter 3), and then proceed to discuss the most common source of translation problem, word meaning (Chapter 4). Topics which are more specifically pedagogical are then explored: the use of dictionaries (Chapter 5); the evaluation of translations and grading of errors (Chapter 6). Finally, there is a summary of strategy tips teachers can give their students and of tips on the grading of errors teachers can use for their marking of translations (Chapter 7).

The book is aimed at teachers of translation who are interested in explaining translation in a rational way. One may, of course, hold the opinion that translating is an intuitive process inspired, perhaps, by the translator's creative gift. But can we teach intuition? We may be able to create an atmosphere favourable to intuition. But when it comes to deciding which of the various ideas that have come to our minds should be chosen, intuition will have to be counterbalanced by reflection, at least if we want to carry conviction with our students. We cannot really hope to rely on arguments of the type, "This is a better translation because I feel it is better." What our students need are rational arguments which, as far as possible, are based on objective principles. Professional translators should know what they are doing, and should be able to talk about it with those who commission translations and with those whose translations they have to supervise or revise. It is the rational approach which distinguishes the expert from the non-expert.

The book, as has been stated, is intended for teachers of translation - primarily. But why should not students read it as well? They might well be able to learn a good deal about translation on their own. Also, after reading the book they may become more like equals to their teachers in discussions. I hope their teachers will appreciate this.

Chapter 1

What goes on in the translator's mind?

1.1 Types of empirical research

How can we teach translation? All of us who are involved in the training of professional translators will have more or less explicit answers to this question. Many of us will refer to our teaching experience and will be able to list a number of problems and suggest ways of dealing with them. And some of us will be able to refer to a theoretical and methodological framework for their practical teaching.

Nevertheless, those of us who are honest will occasionally have asked ourselves: do we really put enough emphasis on the right areas? Or could it be that we stress problems which are not problems for our students after all, and that we actually disregard areas where they encounter difficulties? And has it ever crossed our minds that our students might perhaps have found ways of dealing with problems which we may never have thought of and which, if they are successful, may serve as models for our teaching.

In order to find out more about what goes on in our students' minds, translation teaching ought to be based on data-based research. To my knowledge, there are two of these approaches, product-oriented and process-oriented ones (cf. Toury 1991:45ff.). I shall deal with these approaches in some detail because teachers of translation may want to do their own research.

There is product-oriented error analysis and translation quality assessment. It can be divided into three steps, description of errors (looking at the symptoms), finding the reasons for the errors (diagnosis), and pedagogical help (therapy). The criteria for error description are prospective, i.e. we try to describe the effect the translation, given a specific purpose, produces on the reader. Errors could, for instance, be described as "unjustified narrowing down of the meaning of words, insufficient stylistic precision, lack of textual cohesion" etc. These descriptions form the basis for the grading of errors. I shall discuss this topic in detail in Chapter 6 on "evaluation and errors".

Looking for the reasons of errors has been one of the main concerns of foreign language teaching pedagogy. It is generally assumed that when learning a foreign language we get a mixture of mother tongue and foreign language, a so-called "interlanguage", on the basis of which some errors can be explained (cf. Corder 1973:145ff., 284ff.). They usually result from interferences in a very broad sense as when the learner transfers the phonological, grammatical or lexical system of his mother tongue onto the foreign language. For instance, for the distinction between cognitive and empirical knowledge there are two verbs in German, *wissen* and *kennen,* but in English there is only one verb, *know.* We will therefore not be surprised when an English speaker learning German produces the sentence: *Er kennt nicht was er tun soll* instead of *Er weiß nicht, was er tun soll* (cf. Corder 1973:285).

As teachers of translation we can make use of the interlanguage approach when students translate into the foreign language. But at a more advanced stage these "linguistic" types of errors will decrease, and when translating into the mother tongue they will be comparatively rare anyway. This does not mean, however, that there will not be errors any more. There will still be stylistic errors, errors where the situation of the target readers has not been sufficiently considered, and there will always be errors of comprehension. For these types of errors foreign language error analysis has as yet little to offer. Moreover, diagnoses based on errors are largely speculative, because we can only infer what went on in the translator's mind. Our expectations and guesses may coincide with reality, i.e. with what happens in the translation process, but there are also the well-known cases when we find mistakes in our students' translations which are explained to us by our students in a completely different manner from the way we would have explained them on the basis of our error analysis.

The fact that by looking at the product we can at best speculate about the process that led up to it does not seem to be clear to all who write about this topic. Thus, Hatim and Mason (1990) seem to think that they can actually retrace the pathways of the translator's decision-making procedures by looking at the translated text (p.3/4). Bell (1991) when developing his model of the translation process seems to be aware of the need for introspection and conscious observation of the processes involved in translation in order to complement his model. Nevertheless he presents a model gained by working back from the output (the product) by the logical process of induction (Bell 1991:29, 267). I am not saying that as teachers and instructors we cannot make use of these approaches, but when adopting them we should not raise expectations which cannot be fulfilled. Their value lies not so much in the illumination of the mental processes in translation but rather in their pedagogical function. They can help us to put our students on the right path, as it were, and if they have lost their way these approaches can help them to get a clearer view of their destination again. It will be seen in this chapter that unsuccessful translation processes could, in fact, have been avoided if the translators had been aware and made use of the methods of text analysis and translation criticism while translating. I shall therefore deal with these approaches in more detail in the subsequent chapters.

In order to avoid errors we should prescribe a "therapy". We can advise our students to take courses in mother tongue usage in order to become more sensitive to the way they use their own language. We can also prescribe a remedial course in the foreign language in order to improve their foreign language competence. We can prescribe a course in text analysis in order to improve their understanding of the source text and help them with their decisions when translating it. However, therapies of this sort would be like trying to get someone to find their way through a fog unless we can guide their steps clearly, that is, point out more precisely how students produced their errors.

A new process-oriented approach has been developed recently in order to gain more immediate access to that notorious black box, the translator's mind. By adopting introspective methods from psychology, experiments have been carried out in which translators were asked to utter everything that went on in their minds while they were translating, and these monologues were tape recorded. These monologues are referred to as think-aloud protocols (TAPs). Such protocols have been analysed in order to classify translation strategies, with the pedagogical (diagnostic) aim of observing difficulties encountered by the students. The title of this chapter is, in fact, a translation of the title of the pioneering study in this field by Krings (cf. Krings 1986, cf. also House/Blum-Kulka 1986, Königs 1987, Lörscher 1986, 1991). Although by using TAPs we are "closer" to the translator's mind we still to some extent have to infer what goes on, as we shall see when analysing the protocols. There is no, and probably never will be, direct access to mental processes. But there is, I hope, an improvement by degree when analysing protocols instead of errors.

1.2 Methodological problems with think-aloud protocols

1.2.1 Choice of subjects

TAPs as methods of empirical research into the translation process proper have proved to be a bold step in the right direction and the results gained were often unexpected and sometimes surprising, but the first studies made do not really inform us about professional translating or, indeed, translating as it goes on in translator training institutions. The subjects of the experiments were foreign language students and translating for them was part of their foreign language learning curriculum. Thus the subjects were not told for whom they were supposed to translate, nor for what purpose, that is to say a translation assignment was completely missing. Moreover, they did not have any systematic instructions in how to deal with texts in order to translate them. In their curriculum translation was basically used for testing foreign language skills.

This lack of a methodological basis sometimes becomes painfully obvious in the decision-making strategies of the subjects, for instance of those used by Krings (1986a,b) in his first empirical study. They resorted to such naive principles as "If all competing potential equivalents turn out to be equally appropriate or inappropriate, take the most literal one!" or "Take the shortest one!" or "If one of the equivalents is to be found in the bilingual dictionary and the other one is not, take the one from the dictionary!" or "If all equivalents concerned are in the dictionary, take the one that precedes the others!" (Krings 1986b:273) With the methodological background they had, it is not surprising that the subjects came up with these bizarre principles. What is surprising, though, is that these "strategies", as he calls them, remain uncriticized by Krings. Krings and in fact many of the scholars engaged in protocol research seem to avoid judgements altogether in their studies. They do not link up the decision making strategies they observe with the resulting translations. Lörscher is aware of the fact "that what the subjects consider to be successful and what the analyst does often do not coincide" and that what subjects think to be good solutions apparently are translation errors (Lörscher 1992a:159). Nevertheless, he, in the same way as Krings, does not take this further step and combine analysis and evaluation. In my opinion, there is no reason for this kind of restraint. If we want to provide data for translation teaching, we cannot abstain from evaluating the translations which are produced at the end of the processes observable in the protocols. If the translations are unsatisfactory, then one may with some justification expect that the processes leading up to them are problematic too (cf. Hönig 1988b:11). If the translations are of high quality, the subjects will most likely have used appropriate strategies (cf. Jääskeläinen 1993:112).

It is one of the aims of my investigation to isolate such processes in order to find out where our students have problems and then to help them. This means that in my analysis of the various solution-finding processes I shall always link up process and product, that is I shall evaluate the translations eventually decided on by the subjects, and I shall use the model of communicative error analysis and translation quality assessment described in Chapter 6.

The obvious thing to do, therefore, seems to apply these introspective methods to students training to become professional translators, i.e. semi-professionals. There have been a number of studies of both professionals and semi-professionals recently (cf. Krings 1987, Hönig 1988b, Séguinot (ed.)1989, Kiraly 1990, Gerloff 1988, Lörscher 1992b), and in some of these, professional situations have been at least simulated, i.e. the subjects had had some training and the importance of the translation assignment was realized (cf. Jääskeläinen 1989, 1993 Tirkkonen 1989,1992, Hönig 1988b, Kiraly 1990). It was observed that there are indeed differences between professionals and semi-professionals on the one hand and non-professionals on the other in the way they produce their translations. I shall refer to these studies when presenting my own observations made in seminars.

I am using semi-professionals for my protocols because they represent the typical student in institutions for professional translation training, that is to say a person who has acquired a methodological basis and a certain amount of translation competence but who faces nevertheless still a number of problems when translating. A semi-professional can be compared to a sailor who knows the direction in which he should steer his boat but finds it hard to keep the right course in stormy weather.

Moreover, I do not think there is such a big difference between professionals and semi-professionals. We are all semi-professionals to some extent. Although we may know all the necessary techniques and strategies, we still on occasion fail to make use of them. I have often observed advanced students, including myself, stubbornly sticking to a word, for instance, instead of looking for a paraphrase, and even if we are aware of all the necessary techniques, solutions do not just spring to mind. The reason seems to me that translation is not only a skill but also a problem-solving process. If translation were a skill like, say, driving a car, professionalism could be achieved once and for all. The correct actions for driving can be internalized, and then normal driving situations are mastered without any conscious mental effort. With problem-solving activities like translating, internalization of strategies and techniques is only part of the process. There will always be situations when we have to make a conscious effort, and it is in these situations that we often get the feeling that we are, alas, semi-professionals only.

Professionalism thus is a relative quality, and it might be argued that the distinction between the non-professionals used as subjects by Krings, Königs and Lörscher and the semi-professionals I used is a rather vague one. The distinction is indeed not of a qualitative but a quantitative nature. As Königs pointed out to me (private communication) there may be foreign language students (i.e. non-professionals) who solve problems in a similar way as semi-professionals, and there may be semi-professionals who have the same difficulties with their solution searching processes as non-professionals. Nevertheless, if subjects have been provided with translation strategies there is a greater chance that they will arrive at good solutions. And the instances where, in spite of a knowledge of strategies, they do not arrive at useful solutions will perhaps highlight the bigger problems.

In my analysis of the protocols I shall point out a few of the situations and problems which typically arise. Ideally, such an analysis should be statistically based. Since the corpora of protocols that have been used so far, including my own, are still rather small, it is perhaps too early to make use of statistics. It has been argued by Krings (private communication) that I am focussing on specific points of detail and that I am not presenting a coherent analysis of the corpora, however small, that I have used. He is right, and I would answer that my selection is guided by my observation of errors. I start off with the errors, and I am then trying to find out which types of processes have led up to them. Moreover, I must admit that my observation of errors is influenced by my experience as a teacher of translation, and to those of us who teach, the problems described will, I expect, look familiar. One might even argue that many years of experience in translation teaching or indeed in translating is also a good basis, although not a strictly scientific one, for identifying typical problems. Nevertheless, the observations I present should not be regarded as final truths but rather as hypotheses that ought to be tested by further TAP-studies.

In this chapter, then, I shall describe some problems students have, i.e. unsuccessful processes that take place in their minds, and in the subsequent chapters I hope to present some techniques and strategies that can be used to overcome these problems so that their processes will ultimately prove successful. It has been observed by Krings (private communication) that I am mainly concerned with errors, and he has suggested to me that one should also look for strategies in the TAPs that were successful. My preoccupation with errors may be explained by the fact that I have been a teacher involved in translator training for over twenty years and that I have a pedagogical interest in helping students to avoid them. However, I have also observed students using strategies that led to good, even brilliant solutions, and I have made TAP-analyses of successful ✓ solution-searching processes from the point of view of creativity. In the second Chapter, I shall describe some of these successful processes which might be used as models for teaching purposes.

1.2.2 Elicitation methods

The value of TAPs has recently been questioned. In an empirical study, House(1988) observed that think-aloud in pairs yields richer, more insightful data than think-aloud alone. Whereas monologue protocols contain a large amount of descriptive talk accompanying the action and long stretches of silence and the processes leading up to decisions are often not verbalized, in dialogue protocols solutions are negotiated and thoughts appear to be consistently shaped through the necessity to verbalize them.

I made use of this method almost at the same time as House and can fully corroborate her findings. I would venture the hypothesis that processes which in monologue protocols are unobservable because they remain in a "sub-control workspace", as Kiraly calls it (1990:148), can be brought to the subjects' consciousness in dialogue protocols by the very fact that they ask each other to explain how they have achieved their translations. Kiraly's observation that the actualisation of translational competencies takes place at a subconscious, relatively uncontrolled level (Kiraly 1990:148, 152) may be due to his exclusive use of monologue protocols. It is certainly true that in normal translation situations much of what we do is intuitive and internalized, but the aim of TAPs, after all, is to shed some light on these normally intuitive processes. We should not be satisfied with observing that overt application of rules or strategies is rare in our protocols. We should rather improve or change our experimental techniques so that eventually we do get a glimpse, however short, into the "black box".

With dialogue protocols there is, of course, the additional danger of after-the-event rationalization, i.e. explanations how a translation was achieved. It may very well happen that one of the subjects asks the other: "How did you find this solution? Why do you think this is a good translation?" And when answering such questions the subjects may not describe what actually went on in their minds while translating but what they think is a good argument. When analysing the protocols we should therefore concentrate on processes which lead up to a translation, and we do get this type of pre-event material. For instance, we get discussions about the meaning of a word or phrase within a text or we can observe strings of solutions, one stimulating the other.

I also agree with House that working in pairs has a large pedagogical potential and "teaching translation in and as interaction ...might be preferable to the still overwhelmingly popular practice of asking students to translate in splendid isolation" (House 1988:96). In my seminars, producing dialogue protocols and analysing them proved to be an excellent method for stimulating discussions between students and making them aware of what they were doing with the result that translation in its training stage could become a more rational affair.

One may raise the objection, however, that this kind of experiment does not actually mirror the real life situation, since for financial reasons, professional translating normally involves only one translator. Thus, if we record the teamwork of two translators, we do not observe one mind at work but two, and we might record thoughts that would never have occurred to a single translator. I would argue that we are not interested in a single mind anyway, but in getting a sample of minds. We can thus regard the two subjects whose dialogue we are recording as part of this sample. We must, however, be careful in choosing the subjects that work together. They should have equal or at least comparable translating skills and also equal linguistic and methodological knowledge and an equal ability in expressing themselves.

There is another argument against teamwork which concerns the psychodynamic interaction between partners. It may very well be that one of them takes the leading role not because of his or her superior capabilities, but because of personality features. Also, one of the subjects may hold back his or her ideas for reasons of politeness - or even chivalry. I remember one male student accepting his female partner's translation with the words: "O.K. I won't quibble. You are ✓ the lady on our team." Translations which are decided upon in this way are, of course, useless for our purposes. When analysing the protocols, we must take care that either both subjects take part in the translation-finding process or that one of them brings the process to an end, at least without being impeded by the other's non-topical arguments and influence. I am aware of the difficulties in noticing these factors when analysing the protocols, but I do not see any other possibility at the moment.

These dynamic processes are comparable to those taking place within groups, and it might be a good idea to take into consideration what psychologists and sociologists have to say about this matter. In selecting the subjects for team-work to be recorded we will be well advised to look for "matching" partners, that is, pairs of subjects in which there is no domination of one over the other and where temperaments are fairly similar.

I am in favour of dialogue-protocols. I am not suggesting, however, that we should dismiss monologue-protocols altogether. I have, in fact, used both methods. There may be individuals who, with some practice and warming up, will not find it unnatural to verbalize their interior monologues while translating and whose TAPs will yield relevant data. Both methods of investigation, monologues and dialogues, can be used in a complementary way, and in fact one method may support the other. If, for instance, dialogue protocols reveal that paraphrasing plays an important part in understanding the meaning of a sentence or passage, this observation becomes more valid if think-aloud monologues show the same type of phenomenon.

Both dialogue and monologue protocols belong methodologically to the class of case studies, and the reliability of this type of research has sometimes been questioned, mainly because one case is after all only one case and, one may add, a few cases are only a few. The problem is basically a statistical one, namely choosing the right sample. As far as this problem is concerned, I can at least say that the subjects chosen in our seminar were at the same (intermediate) stage of their training. They all had had the opportunity of familiarizing themselves with a theoretical model of translation and to apply it to practical translation work. They thus differed significantly from the foreign language students used as subjects in the experiments mentioned above. A certain degree of reflection on what they were doing could be presupposed.

1.2.3 *Explanatory models and text material*

In the following sections I shall describe a number of unsuccessful processes I observed when analysing the protocols. In my analysis I shall refer to explanatory models, specifically psycholinguistic models of comprehension, such as the interaction between *bottom-up and top-down processes* (cf. section 1.2.1). These terms are now common notions in psycholinguistics (cf. Hörmann 1981:124ff.). They seem to have been adopted from artificial intelligence research where they have been used in computer science (cf. Bobrow & Brown 1975). Briefly, they work on assumptions which are very neatly expressed by Jean Aitchison:

> People do not passively 'register' the sentences uttered by a speaker. Instead they hear what they *expect* to hear. They actively reconstruct both the sounds and syntax of an utterance in accordance with their expectations (Aitchison 1976:178).

And, it may be added, not only the syntax but also the meanings of the words of an utterance.

There is another linguistic model which is of explanatory value especially when complex mental entities have to be taken into account. I am referring to Fillmore's *scenes and frames theory* (Fillmore 1976, 1977a, 1977b), which is based on prototype semantics, and has recently been applied to translation (cf. Vannerem/ Snell-Hornby 1986, Snell-Hornby 1988:79ff., Vermeer/Witte 1990, passim, Neubert/Shreve 1992:59f.). In its interpretation of linguistic utterances it relies very much on people's experiences of the world and on their experience of the text they read or hear. Words and phrases in a text (=*frames* in Fillmore's terminology) activate mental pictures (=*scenes* in Fillmore's terminology) in the minds of the readers, which are part of a scene or situation they have known for some time or which has previously been activated by that text. Fillmore uses his model for explaining word meaning, but it can also, and perhaps even more profitably, be used for explaining other types of meaning such as situational and pragmatic meaning, as we shall see in Chapter 3.

In psycholinguistic literature there are also other terms which have been used to refer to the mental processes of understanding. Instead of bottom-up and top-down processes the terms *construction process* and *utilization process* have been used (cf. Clark & Clark 1977:45ff., 450ff.). There may be subtle differences in the meaning of these pairs of terms, but the basic idea expressed through them is the same, namely that in comprehension we compare the meaning of linguistic forms against our mental representations of reality (cf. Clark & Clark1977:452ff.). I prefer to use the terms bottom-up and top-down processes because they are metaphors which quite vividly suggest the mental scenes in Fillmore's sense.

Instead of *scene* we may come across the term *schema* and *script,* which are discussed in Tannen (1979:137-146) and applied to translation by Bell (1991:249ff.). I shall not report the discussion here and explain the rather subtle distinctions in psycholinguistic terminology. For our purposes Fillmore's metaphorical terms and the way he uses them appear to be very helpful. The term *frame,* which has been used before by anthropologists such as Goffman and Hymes, suggests that linguistic forms have no meaning on their own. They are only the frames that have to be filled in by the listeners or readers with a "picture", i.e. the material stored in their memories. Frames are not the complete thing, but they nevertheless "limit" or determine the amount and quality of material to be retrieved from our memory. Pictures must "fit" their frames. If they do not, misunderstandings may occur. The term *scene* suggests that meaning cannot simply be conceived as a set of abstract semantic or situational features but as a holistic experiential notion. Meaning is something perceived in the mind's eye, as it were.

Fillmore's *scenes* and *frames* are comparable to *top-down* and *bottom-up* processes. "Top-down" can be described as "from scene to frame", and "bottom-up" as "from frame to scene". I make additional use of Fillmore's terms in this book because their metaphorical quality helps us to see things in greater detail.

When evaluating the translations found in the protocols I shall make use of a model of translation criticism which is based on a pragmatic variety of text linguistics and which puts its main emphasis on the function of a given word, phrase or passage within a larger context and on the effect it has for a reader in a specific situation within a specific culture. This functional approach is, in fact, very close to the psycholinguistic approach. The only difference is in point of view. Functional text linguistics is focused on utterances and texts with regard to their effects on hearers and readers. Psycholinguistics is focused on the hearer and reader with regard to their comprehension of an utterance or text. The functional text-linguistic approach will be seen to form the basis of the whole book, and it will become especially evident in Chapter 6 on "Evaluation and errors."

There is, of course, the hermeneutic problem that we will only observe facts which fit in with the models we apply. We only observe what, in a way, we already know. It may very well be that our subjects face other problems than those explicable by *bottom-up and top-down processes,* and there may be other ways of evaluating their translations than functional criticism. I may be accused of screening the facts in my protocols, of limiting my range of observation by using specific types of models. I can only say that such screening is intended. In my teaching experience psycholinguistic models do have great explanatory power, and a functional approach to translation criticism does help to produce texts that can be used in actual professional communication.

An awareness of psycholinguistic models seems to be lacking in some of the studies which have been made. Thus Tirkkonen-Condit when talking about the professional translator uses a somewhat problematic category which she calls "non-linguistic interpretation" (Tirkkonen-Condit 1989: 84) and in which the subject relies on encyclopaedic knowledge. From psycholinguistic studies of the process of understanding it should be clear that there is no division between linguistic and extralinguistic knowledge. Top-down processes, which are complemented by bottom-up processes, are in principle not only based on linguistic knowledge from previous parts of the text but also on world knowledge and experience (cf. Hörmann 1981:123ff.).

For my investigations I used five texts with an average length of 160 words in a number of seminars. They belonged to the category of non-fiction and covered a variety of topics, namely education, psychology, cultural anthropology, general semantics and politics. The presentation of the topics was predominantly informative and non-technical, and their informative value was such that an assignment of a translation into German could at least be simulated. Some of the texts had in fact been translated and published in Germany. The texts were used more than once, i.e. several subjects were asked to produce protocols of one and the same text. Thus, when analysing the protocols I could compare the data and had thus a chance of recognizing phenomena more easily. There were eight think-aloud protocols (i.e. monologues) and seven dialogue protocols used as a basis for observation.

When presenting my findings I shall, of course, refer to TAP studies made by others, and it will be seen that at least for some of my observations there is a broader empirical basis.

1.3 Some unsuccessful mental processes: Symptoms and diagnoses

1.3.1 *Interferences*

In our teaching of translation we all have come across a large number of errors and deficiencies, and I do not think I shall be able to add new ones to these lists, but what I hope to do is shed some light on the processes which led up to them.

Let me begin with interferences, which is, in fact, a "diagnostic" notion offering an explanation for special types of errors. Interferences are known to cause howlers. Notorious candidates for causing this type of error are "false friends". There are two types: those which always turn out to be false friends, and those which can sometimes be good friends. The first type includes such words as English *sensible, fabric, eventual*, which can never be translated into German by *sensibel, Fabrik* and *eventuell*. These cause problems for those translators for whom translating is nothing but a linguistic reflex, and for those who do not know when they must switch from automatic reflex to conscious reflection (cf. Hönig 1986).

The second type includes words such as English *psychological, control,* and *drugs* , which can in certain contexts indeed be translated into German by *psychologisch, kontrollieren,* and *Drogen* , but not in all. There is a large number of these untrustworthy friends in European languages. Usually they have a common Latin or Greek root. Other English words of this type which may lead to interferences when translated into German are: *schizoid, cynicism, liberal, melancholy, sanguine, creative, aggressive, structure, institution* (cf. Stein 1980). These words are problems even when translators have already switched to reflection, for they have to decide if the formally corresponding word is the correct translation or if they must look for a formally non-corresponding expression, a decision which sometimes requires a detailed semantic analysis of the context. Semantically speaking, the problem is caused by polysemy. One of the meanings of these words, but not all, can be translated by a formally corresponding TL-word. Thus *drug* in the meaning of "a substance one takes, especially as a habit, for pleasure or excitement" (DCE) can be translated by German "Drogen", but in the meaning of "a medicine or a substance used for making medicines" (DCE) it cannot, but must be translated by "Medikament", "Arznei", or "Medizin".

Since interferences of the first type are caused by a lack of reflection on the part of the translator, naturally no verbalization appears in the protocols. Interferences of this type arise spontaneously and without any comment, which shows that the problem was not realized at all. For the explanation or diagnosis of this type, protocols are therefore of no value and one has to resort to contrastive linguistics and error analysis.

It is the second type for which protocols might be expected to yield some diagnostic insight. Although decision-making processes as such for or against the formally corresponding word could not be observed in the data I used, it became evident that the subjects were often not aware of the danger of interference because they were engaged in solving a problem in the immediate textual neighbourhood of the false friend. This can be seen in the following example, the translation of a text about the physiological processes during sleep:

> (1) Even the brain is growing and repairing itself during sleep, and while it is doing this the blood supply to the brain increases and a person goes through a more wakeful period of dreaming sleep.

> *(The Sunday Times Magazine, September 3, 1980)*

In the TAP protocol we find:

> (The subject is reading the second part of the English sentence) ...und wie sagt man im Deutschen für "a more wakeful period of dreaming sleep"? (Long pause)

Ich mache das jetzt halt ganz frei. (Subject writes down translation.) "Und man kommt in eine Periode, in der der Schlaf leicht ist und man träumt."

Back-translation into English:

... and what do we say in German for "a more wakeful period of dreaming sleep"? (Long Pause) I think I'll do this freely. (Subject writes down the translation) "And one enters a period in which sleep is light and in one dreams".

The problem here was the translation of "period" by German "Periode". In describing the symptoms we may say that in connection with "Schlaf" the German word "Phase" would have been a better collocation. Although the reader will be able to grasp the meaning here the phrasing is not quite idiomatic and will impair the overall linguistic quality of the text. For a diagnosis I would suggest that the obligatory shift (for the term see Catford 1965:73ff.) when translating "more wakeful" and "dreaming sleep" apparently took up so much of the subject's attention that no thoughts were left for the translation of "period". This is perhaps a typical phenomenon. It is well-known that translation problems are not evenly spread over a text. There are passages where things move smoothly and quickly, and there are passages where problems accumulate and where a large number of different types of decisions are called for. Such passages can only be disentangled bit by bit. In these cases the concept of a "multiple stage translation" may be helpful (cf. the discussion in Wilss 1977:268ff.). For practical purposes this would mean that translations have to be checked and revised. The principal problem, however, is recognizing weak points in the first place.

Turning to remedies, in our present case a knowledge of the principle of collocation might be helpful. In my experience a knowledge of certain linguistic principles and methods does indeed help to identify problems and maybe also to solve them. The translators here should have been more aware of the fact that collocations differ between languages. It should be the task of contrastive linguistics to provide methods and the task of lexicography to provide material for this problem area. The biggest problem, however, is that a translator without sufficient linguistic sensitivity will not notice these things at all. The only advice that can be given is to improve one's linguistic competence both in the mother tongue and in the foreign language.

1.3.2 *Fear of interferences*

We can observe interferences both in novices and in advanced translators. Advanced translators, however, often seem to show a kind of overreaction to false friends. If the opportunity arose of translating a false friend of the second type with a formally corresponding word, such as English "passable" by German "passabel", the subjects seemed to be afraid of doing so, and desperately tried to find a solution which showed no formal similarities with the source language word. This happened in the translation of the following text:

> (2)"For one who knows no language but his own" said the late Professor Warner Fite, "the correspondence of words and things is an assumption almost inevitable. For him then the words are not merely conventional symbols for things but real properties of things ... It is then a disillusionment to discover, upon learning a foreign language, that what can be expressed in a word in one tongue requires a pair of words or a whole phrase in another, and that between no two languages is there more than a rather loose correspondence of word to word. This wrenches the word loose from the thing: it introduces what is for me the most characteristic product of philosophical reflection; namely, a consciousness of the variety of human points of view.
>
> (S.I. Hayakawa. *Symbol, Status, and Personality*. New York 1953,.20)

The sentence "It is then a disillusionment..." was at first paraphrased by one of the subjects in the dialogue-protocol by

> ...dann tritt irgendwann die große Desillusionierung ein, wenn man halt erkennt, daß man nicht einfach, zack, ein Wort hier durch ein Wort dort ersetzen kann.

English translation:

> ...then at some time or other there is the great disillusionment, when we cannot but notice, that we can't simply substitute a word here by a word there

In the ensuing discussion between the subjects, however, "Desillusionierung" was not taken into consideration, and it was only after their failure to find some other equivalent word, and after "Desillusionierung" was offered to them by the dictionary, that they eventually made use of it, but not without distinctly expressing their dissatisfaction:

> A: Ja, das gefällt mir zwar noch nicht so ganz mit der Desillusionierung, aber ich weiß nichts besseres.
> B: Das ist jetzt so ein Fall, wo man sich mit der Lösung zufriedengeben muß, nur weil man keine bessere weiß.

English Translation:

> A: Well, I don't quite like "Desillusionierung" here, but I can't think of anything better.
> B: This is a typical case where one has to be satisfied with a solution for the simple reason that one cannot think of a better one.

This dissatisfaction seemed to have been so strong that for their final version the subjects rejected "Desillusionierung" and wrote:

Jeder Fremdsprachenlerner wird dennoch unweigerlich erkennen müssen...

Back-translation into English:

Each learner of a foreign language will inevitably have to realize...

The subjects eventually tried to render "disillusionment" by "unweigerlich erkennen müssen", thereby, no doubt, displaying some shifting skills, but considering the fact that the text here describes a rather painful experience of the naive language user, as can be seen from line 11 ("wrenches the word loose from the thing"), "Desillusionierung", to my mind, would have been the more appropriate word.

I would venture the hypothesis that at the root of the subjects' dissatisfaction was their fear of "false friends". They must have learnt that in many cases the formally similar word in the target language leads to "big blunders", and they will most likely have been warned of these by their teachers. Hönig in his empirical studies has made similar observations (1988:12), and fear of interferences seems indeed to be part of the mental make-up of semi-professionals.

The reason for this may be found in an attitude where individual parts of the text become more important than the text as a whole. Basically, we have here an imbalance between top-down and bottom-up processes. The subjects disregarded the subsequent context (line 9: "wrench") which would have made it clear to them that in "disillusionment" the feature "painfulness of the process" was implied, and thus the bottom-up processes were impeded. Instead, they relied on their idiosyncratic top-down processes which for them seemed to have taken the form of a rule such as: "When translating never use the formally corresponding word!" The internalization of such a rule may, in fact, have been caused by their teachers. There is a long tradition in foreign language and also in translation teaching to warn students of false friends and ensuing interferences. Although teaching experience shows that interferences are typical causes for mistranslations warnings of them may lead to a general insecurity with the effect that students do not dare to look beyond the word-border. Such warnings should therefore always be counterbalanced by contextual considerations.

Just as in the case of interferences students should, by way of therapy, be made aware of the necessary balance between top-down and bottom-up processes and, if necessary, bottom-up processes should be encouraged. This can be done by providing the tools for text analysis (cf. Chapters 2, 3 and 4). In our example the larger verbal context is relevant for the analysis of the referential meaning of "disillusionment". The stylistic meaning of the word can be assessed by pragmatic considerations, that is by taking into account the text-receptor, i.e. the reader of the text, and the text type. In an academic textbook of this kind, the use of "hard" words like German "Desillusionierung" would be wholly appropriate. Lexical decisions in connection with the second type of interference where, when translating into German, we have to decide between an often stylistically marked loan-word and a "German" word, are a chance to demonstrate the value of pragmatic dimensions in text analysis (cf. Chapter 3).

Pragmatic considerations, as Jääskeläinen has shown, are frequent in the protocols of professional translators and advanced students of translation who seem to use "global strategies" when making decisions (Jääskeläinen 1993:113ff.). It would seem then that as teachers we should provide these overall strategies. This exactly is the purpose of this book.

1.3.3 Faulty one-to-one correspondences

Learners of a foreign language and translators are often not aware of the fact that words might have more meanings than the meaning they know. This can be shown in the translation of the newspaper-report quoted above (1) about sleep and the human body.

> (3) Good sleep is essential for this process of bodily renewal, and if people are deprived of sleep for a number of nights then they lose their ability to concentrate. Inability to sleep properly may be a sign that a person is worried, depressed, drinking too much or taking insufficient exercise. The majority of people who complain about their inability to sleep properly are worriers.
> (*The Sunday Times Magazine*, September 3, 1980)

The problem for the subject was the translation of "deprived of sleep". In the TAP we read:

> ..."and" - diesen Anschluß halte ich nicht für gut. Im Englischen steht oft "and", ich glaube aber, das ist hier kausal; deshalb setze ich "denn" ein. ... "people are deprived of sleep" - "beraubt sein" ist eine zu hohe Stilebene, also "entzogen sein" ... "people" - wird das im Deutschen mit Singular oder Plural wiedergegeben? "Wenn einem Menschen" - "Wenn Menschen" - ich würde es im Singular schreiben.

English translation:

> ..."and" - I don't think this is a good connective. "And" is very common in English texts. The relationship here, I think, is causal; therefore I shall write "denn" (for). ... "People are deprived of sleep" - German "beraubt sein" sounds too elevated stylistically; I shall use "entzogen sein" instead ... "people" - do I have to render this with a singular or a plural form in German "Wenn einem Menschen" (if a person) - "wenn Menschen" (if people) - I think I'll use the singular.

The written translation ran as follows:

> Ein gesunder Schlaf ist für diesen Prozess der körperlichen Erneuerung unbedingt notwendig, denn ein Mensch, dem mehrere Nächte lang der Schlaf entzogen wird, verliert seine Konzentrationsfähigkeit.

As in the case of example (1) the subject feels she is faced with a cluster of problems. I shall not comment on the appropriateness of the subject's categories of analysis and decision-making. The important thing to be noticed is that in this short passage the subject is faced with a variety of problems, including syntactic, stylistic and grammatical ones, which may be the reason why "deprived of" was mistranslated. "Entzogen" implies that there is an external force, but the reasons for the sleeping problems mentioned in the text, as is evident from the lines that follow, are not external but internal ones. A more adequate translation would have been "Wer mehrere Nächte lang nicht schlafen kann..."

Broadly speaking, the error can be explained as sign-oriented translating, a typical behaviour, as Lörscher observed, in foreign language learners (Lörscher 1991:272-274, Lörscher 1992a:153). More specifically, what happened here was that the subject had stored one meaning in his memory, but she did not notice that this meaning did not make sense in the context in front of her. This failure can be explained by Königs' concept of a learning-induced one-to-one-correspondence "lerngeleitete 1:1-Entsprechung" (Königs 1987:168, cf. also Krings 1986: 271 for a similar explanation). The learner of a foreign language has internalized the most common and frequent meaning of a word but not all of its potential meanings. Very often these "unknown" meanings are figurative ones. The semantic reason for this error can be seen in the fact that the word in question is polysemous, but in this case, in contrast to interference, there is no formal correspondence when rendering one of the meanings of the SL-word by a TL-word.

It was noticed by Königs and also by Krings and Lörscher that this type of mistake was common among their subjects who were foreign language students (cf. Königs 1987:168ff., Krings 1987:271, Lörscher 1992a:153). It could be argued that our semi-professional subject here shows non-professional features typical of language learners and that this type of mistake is caused by insufficient lexical knowledge in the foreign language. One may feel tempted to recommend that the student enlarge his or her foreign language competence.

To my mind the underlying idea that a foreign language competence can be enlarged and improved until it reaches a stage of completion rests on a misconception of what goes on in the process of understanding words in texts. I do not think one will ever be able to reach a stage where one's competence is large enough to cover all possible semantic uses of words. As we shall see in the section about meaning and the use of dictionaries (Chapter 5), there will always be situations where in a given text we will come across meanings of words which we have never encountered before.

In addition to the advice that one should improve one's foreign language competence I would suggest that teachers should try to make students aware of what goes on in their minds during the process of understanding so that eventually they may internalize these processes. They will then acquire the behaviour which Lörscher in his empirical work observed with professional translators who took a sense-oriented approach to translation (Lörscher 1992a:154,). More specifically, as I shall show below (Chapters 3, 4 and 5), words take on meaning in texts (a) by their meaning potential and (b) by the context which activates, determines and limits their meaning potential. On the part of the hearer or reader two types of processes take place. He builds up a hypothesis about the meaning of a word on the basis of his knowledge either stored in his memory or gained from the previous context (= the top-down process), which is then tested against the actual utterances he hears or the actual text in front of him (= the bottom-up process). Only if there is a balance between these processes does understanding function smoothly. If there is not, we run the risk of misunderstanding an utterance or a text.

In our example the subject relied too heavily on the (incomplete) potential meaning of "deprived", stored in her memory, and she did not take enough notice of the actual text in which "deprived" was used and which would have made it clear to her that the meaning stored in her mind for this word was not comprehensive enough. In other words, bottom-up processes were blotted out by top-down processes. For cases such as this I would recommend that we make our students aware of the important role of context in the activation of word meaning (cf. Chapters 3 and 4).

1.3.4 *Misuse of bilingual dictionaries*

The predominance of top-down processes is sometimes increased by relying too much on bilingual dictionaries. In the text by Hayakawa quoted above (2) the sentence

> For him then words are not merely conventional symbols for things but real properties of things"

was commented as follows:

> A: Für ihn sind die Worte nicht einfach nur - kann man "konventionell" sagen?
> B: Konventionell, konventionell -
> A: Konventionell - denkt man immer an Rüstung und Waffen
> B: Ja, herkömmliche Symbole, konventionell ist eigentlich herkömmlich, ne?
> ...

A: Ich guck mal, was unter "conventional" steht. - Das ist gut: "conventional: konventionell, konventionsgebunden, herkömmlich, traditionell, normalerweise üblich", steht hier im Zusammenhang mit "symbols" oder "mealtimes", "normalerweise üblich". "It is conventional to do something: Es ist normalerweise üblich, etwas zu tun". Paßt das denn? Oder einfach "sind nur die üblichen Symbole".

B: Ja genau, also das ist gar nicht so wichtig, das "conventional." Es kommt ja auf das "symbol" an.

...

oder "Für ihn waren die Worte nicht nur die üblichen Symbole, sondern die Sache selbst."

A: Machen wir so!

English translation:

A: For him words are not merely - can one say "konventionell"?
B: "Konventionell, konventionell" -
A: "Konventionell" - one immediately thinks of arms
B: Yes; "herkömmliche Symbole", "konventionell" is the same as "herkömmlich" actually, don't you think
A: I'll have a look what the dictionary says for conventional". That's not bad. "Conventional: konventionell, konventionsgebunden, herkömmlich, traditionell, normalerweise üblich"; it is seen here in connection with "symbols" or "mealtimes", "normalerweise üblich". "It is conventional to do something: Es ist normalerweise üblich etwas zu tun". Does this fit? Or simply "sind nur die üblichen Symbole".
B: Yes, exactly. "Conventional" here is not so important after all. The emphasis is on "symbol".

...

Or: "Für ihn waren die Worte nicht nur die üblichen Symbole, sondern die Sache selbst." (back-translation: For him words were not merely the usual symbols but the very things themselves)
A: We'll leave it at that!

German "konventionell" is immediately associated by one of the subjects with "Rüstung und Waffen", a semantically restricted use, caused by the subject's incomplete competence in her mother tongue. By this faulty top-down process the use of "konventionell", which would have been the appropriate linguistic technical term in this context, is blocked. There is another typical type of behaviour which can be observed in this sentence. In the subjects' first paraphrase of the sentence, "conventional" was not translated at all:

Worte sind nicht nur Symbole, sondern die Sache selbst.(Words are not only symbols for things but they indeed are the things)

The subjects seem to have recognized that in this sentence the contrast between "symbols" and "real properties" was the main point. This also becomes apparent in B's comment "also das ist gar nicht so wichtig". Paradoxically though, "üblich" was preserved in the end version. This wavering between correct contextualization in the process of understanding and a sticking-to-the-word attitude seems to be typical for our semi-professionals. It could also be observed in the translation of "disillusionment" described above, and the psycholinguistic reason for it can again be seen in the imbalance between top-down and bottom-up processes.

Very often this behaviour goes together with a belief in the dictionary as the final authority. The protocol quoted is a case in point. The technical linguistic meaning of "conventional" could, of course, not be expected to be found in a general bilingual dictionary, and here also the collocation with "symbol", mentioned and translated in the dictionary by "normalerweise üblich", was definitely misleading. Nevertheless, meaning inferred from context should have been given priority over meaning gained from the dictionary; in this case the recognition that "conventional" in this context was basically redundant should have been adhered to for the final version.

My observations are corroborated by those made by Hönig (1988:1991). He found that his semi-professional subjects often correctly inferred the meaning of a word from its context, but when they could not find the meaning in their dictionaries they did not have the courage to adhere to it. Hönig's suggestion is to build up students' self-confidence so that they will rely on their understanding of the text rather than on a dictionary, which of course implies that they have acquired strategies of understanding, which again can be taught (cf. Hönig 1988b:12; Hönig 1991:87f.). I fully agree, and I would add that an awareness of the psycholinguistic processes of understanding might be helpful for students in this respect.

There are additional dangers in the use of bilingual dictionaries. By their very nature they immediately present us with target language equivalences (cf. Chapter 5, section 5.1). If we use them for translation purposes, the phase of abstraction, where we detach ourselves from the wording of a text, is completely suppressed, and the possibilities of finding adequate translations for specific contexts by using our own imagination are very much reduced.

In translation teaching, at least when translating from the foreign language into the mother tongue, the use of monolingual dictionaries should be strongly recommended (cf. Chapter 5). Their superior qualities can be demonstrated by a further example taken from the Hayakawa text. The phrase "the late professor Warner Fite" was handled by our subjects in the following way:

> B: Ja, "late professor" - Guck mal nach, guck mal unter "late" nach.
> A: Gut.(schlägt in *Pons Globalwörterbuch Englisch-Deutsch* nach)
>   "Verstorben!"

B: Ah.
A: Ja, "früher" kann man bei einem Professor wohl kaum sagen. "Verstorben" steht hier "the late John F. Kennedy".
B: Hm. Gut. Ja.

English translation:

B: Well, "late professor" - Let's have a look under "late".
A: All right. (Looks up word in *Pons Globalwörterbuch Englisch-Deutsch*) "Verstorben"
B: I see.
A: Hm, one can't very well say "früher" with a professor. "Verstorben" it says here "the late John F. Kennedy".
B: Hm. Okay. All right then.

Here again, the information of the bilingual dictionary is misleading. "Late" does have a meaning that can be rendered by "verstorben" but not in this context. In German and also in English it is unconventional to specify when a person has died unless the death has occurred quite recently, and as Hayakawa's essay was published in 1953, but our translation was done as late as 1987, the professor's death, then, was not exactly a recent event. The information about the length of the time span, lacking in the bilingual dictionary, can be found in a monolingual dictionary, such as the DCE:

who has died recently: her late husband/the late president

The distinctive semantic feature of "late" for our context is "recently", which also becomes apparent in the example given. If our subjects had used this kind of information together with the pragmatic consideration that there is a long time span between the professor's death and the translation of our text, they might have realized that "late" here would have to remain untranslated. There may then be some conflict between "literal" translation and translation which takes account of broader social, cultural and historical considerations, the latter undoubtedly being preferable. This question is taken up again in sections 3.1 - 3.3.

1.3.5 *Misuse of world knowledge and one's own experiences*

Preconceived ideas based on top-down processes, about the meanings of words were one of the reasons for the mistranslations mentioned in the previous sections. Preconceived ideas are, of course, not restricted to the meanings of individual words. Thus the subjects engaged in the translation of the Hayakawa-text associated its ideas all too quickly with their own experience as translators. In

Fillmore's terms, they associated a much too idiosyncratic scene:

> A: Aha, das ist das, daß man bei Übersetzungen nicht immer Wort-zu-Wort-Entsprechungen findet.
> B: Genau, genau, ja, ja.
> A: Und daß es eben, daß es immer nur mehr oder weniger vage Entsprechungen gibt, also von einem Wort in den verschiedenen Sprachen, das ist der zweite Teil, daß eben ein Wort in der einen Sprache nicht hundertprozentig mit der anderen Sprache übereinstimmt ... daß ein Wort - vielleicht kann man hier Ausgangssprache und Zielsprache reinbringen - daß ein Wort der Ausgangssprache oft nur durch mehrere Wörter der Zielsprache wiedergegeben werden kann.
> B: Ja, das wäre noch deutlicher ... "beim Übersetzen" ist gut, das macht das ziemlich deutlich, das war gut.

English translation:

> A: I see, this means that when translating one doesn't always find word-to-word-correspondences.
> B: Yes, exactly.
> A: And that there can only be more or less vague equivalents, I mean for words in different languages, the idea of the second part of the passage is, that words in one language don't completely correspond with words in another language ... that a word - maybe we can use source-language and target-language here - that a word in the source-language must often be rendered by several words in the target language.
> B: Yes, this would make things even clearer ... "beim Übersetzen" - that's a good idea, makes things very clear, good idea.

A translator will, no doubt, be able to have the experience described in the text by Hayakawa, but this specific interpretation also means restricting the information given. The realization that there are differences in the structures of two languages can be made in many foreign language learning situations and not only when translating. The rather special interpretation presented by our subjects does not exactly lead to a complete distortion of the meaning of the text, but the dangers of relying too heavily on top-down processing in understanding texts become, I think, apparent from this example. If the subjects had been more text-analytical, they would have found out that Hayakawa was not addressing translators but the general public interested in practical semantics, and for this readership language learning- experiences are more vivid than translation experiences. Pragmatic text analysis thus would here have helped to achieve the necessary balance between top-down and bottom-up processing.

In another (monologue) protocol on the translation of a satirical text about food in British motorway restaurants the message was completely distorted because of the all too subjective associations of the translator. In understanding the sentence "Starch is cheap and filling, so sausages composed chiefly of bread seem somehow right" the subject made use of her own knowledge about food in German snack-bars and translated the second part of the sentence by "Hot dogs mit viel Brot" or alternatively "Würstchen mit Baguette". In this example, a "scene" which the subject had experienced was much too dominant in her mind, in other words, top-down processes blotted out bottom-up processes completely.

Top-down processes may help in the correct understanding of an utterance but at the same time they can lead students astray if they are not counterbalanced by bottom-up processes at every single moment. In one of my translation classes a student had to translate a passage from Hatim and Mason's book, *Discourse and the Translator* (1991) into German. She found that the sentence

> (4) Our ability to recognize texts as instances of a type - exposition, argumentation, instruction - depends on our experience of previous instances of the same type, in other words, on our ability to recognize texts as signs. (p.2)

reminded her of the text-typology of Reiss (1971), which distinguishes between "Darstellung", "Ausdruck" and "Appell", and she thus translated the sentence by

> Unsere Fähigkeit, Texte als Beispiele eines Typs zu erkennen - Darstellung, Argumentation und Appell - ...

Top-down processes were helpful here, but only to a certain point. "Darstellung" is a good equivalent for "exposition", and a person not acquainted with the typology proposed by Reiss might not have found this expression so easily. Our student was also careful enough to retain "Argumentation" and not replace it by "Ausdruck", which would have distorted the meaning of the sentence. She thus counterbalanced top-down by bottom-up processing. But when translating "instruction" by "Appell" she missed the mark. Here Reiss's term seems to have been overwhelmingly present in her mind, and no room seems to have been left in her brain for comparing the meanings of "instruction" and "Appell".

One might argue that the different types of texts mentioned here merely serve as examples and that "Appell" therefore is just as good as "Instruktion". If our sentence was an isolated statement, this would be true. But if seen in the context of the whole book where the authors later on explicitly distinguish between instruction and the categories suggested by Reiss, we must be more precise. Moreover, this precision is especially important in an academic textbook, where different points of view of various scholars are discussed. As translators we must thus be aware that sentences must be seen in the context of larger entities, and these entities have specific pragmatic functions.

This type of text analysis is part of the bottom-up processes, and the switching over to them which would have been necessary here might have been achieved by a more critical attitude toward the translator's own thought processes. In single language communication this critical attitude will be asked for only occasionally in order to avoid misunderstanding. Normally, processes of understandingwork automatically. But in translation a greater awareness of these processes seems to be of paramount importance.

The observations I have made are very similar to those of Tirkkonen-Condit in a TAP study of a professional and a non-professional translator. She found that "the non-professional translator ... resorts to extra-textual world knowledge rather than knowledge extracted from the text. Her main concern is with "truth" rather than with what is said in the text" (Tirkkonen-Condit 1992:439) As a result, the non-professional translator's attitude toward the text seemed to be "more arrogant" and not as modest as that of the professional (Tirkkonen-Condit 1992:439). Tirkkonen-Condit's findings thus seem to corroborate my observations, namely that an imbalance between bottom-up and top-down processes is typical of the approach of the non-professional.

1.3.6 Incomplete paraphrasing

It was observed by Krings (1986:509) in his study of the mental processes in action during translation that intralingual paraphrase operations, within the source or target language, are probably the most frequent means of finding interlingual equivalents. Lörscher (1986:290f.) and Königs (1991:134ff.) found that rephrases of segments of the mother tongue source text were used to arrive at target language forms. These findings are not surprising, since the ability to free oneself from the fetters of a source-language segment seems to be one of the most basic techniques in translating. It is the process central to Seleskovitch's work on interpreting (cf. for instance 1976:103), and it is usually referred to as "translation shifts" or "transpositions" in translation studies (for the terms see Wilss 1982:101f.), and paraphrasing can indeed be regarded as a type of shift. Fleischmann (1991), who listened to oral translations of professional translators from German into Russian found that they used paraphrasing efficiently when they could not find direct equivalents and regarded their paraphrases as proper translations. The semi-professionals, however, whom I observed in my case-studies had a somewhat ambivalent and peculiar attitude toward paraphrasing which impeded their solution-finding processes. They did use paraphrasing in order to get access to the meaning of a sentence, but strangely enough, they did not carry through with their method to the final solution. In the Hayakawa-text, quoted above, the sentence

> For him then words are not merely conventional symbols for things but real properties of things

was, after some preliminary discussion of the meaning and translation of individual words, paraphrased and summarized in German in the following way:

> Also gemeint ist: Worte sind nicht nur Symbole dafür, sondern sind die Sache selbst. (Well then, this means: words are not just symbols for things, they indeed are the things)

This paraphrase was preserved right through to the final version, which ran:

> Für ihn sind die Worte nicht nur die üblichen Symbole für eine Sache. Sie sind die Sache selbst.

I have already discussed and criticized the translation of "conventional" by "üblich". What I want to point out now is that the translators seem to have acquired the basic skill of producing shifts or transpositions, namely the mental flexibility for separating words from their meanings and expressing the meaning in different but semantically still appropriate grammatical forms and syntactic structures. My observations are corroborated by the findings of Lörscher who notes: "The translator often systematically endeavours to make the meaning of SL text segments explicit by separating it from the forms used to express it" (Lörscher 1986:290, cf. also Lörscher 1992a:153f.).

What makes these processes only partly successful in the present case is that the subjects are still preoccupied with the meaning of "conventional", which they separate from the context, as we have seen in the section on the misuse of bilingual dictionaries, and thus arrive at an inadequate translation ("Für ihn waren die Worte nicht nur die üblichen Symbole, sondern die Sache selbst"). Thus the full potential of paraphrasing is not made use of. There is another instance of this phenomenon in our text. The first sentence

> For one who knows no language but his own ...the correspondence of words and things is an assumption almost inevitable

was initially translated (via paraphrasing) by the subjects as:

> Für denjenigen der nur seine eigene Sprache kennt, entsprechen die Worte automatisch den Dingen. (Back-translation: For one who knows no language but his own words automatically correspond to things)

The final version, however, was for no obvious reason linked up much more closely with the original:

> Jemand, der nur seine eigene Sprache kennt, geht fast immer von einer Entsprechung zwischen Worten und Dingen aus. (Back-translation: A person who knows no language but his own will almost always assume that there is a correspondence between words and things.)

This version is still based on some shifting ("assumption almost inevitable" -

"geht fast immer...aus"), but the language user's naive attitude, implicit in "almost inevitable" and very well expressed by "automatisch" in the first translation, is lost in the final translation. On the one hand, the students do have the capability of freeing themselves from the fetters of a literal version, but on the other hand they quite often seem to lack the courage to stick to their "free" version. Once again the individual word seems to become the focus of attention.

There is an even more striking example in another (monologue) protocol. The text specimen to be translated was taken from an article about job dissatisfaction.

> (5) Waking up was the worst part, that minute when at seven a.m. I snapped out of a shallow sleep and instantly reviewed what the day would bring. The suggestions and decisions I would be required to make, the ideas I must generate, the stack of phone calls to be returned and letters to be answered. (*Cosmopolitan*, September 1983)

In the protocol referring to the last sentence we read:

> ...also sie muß halt Ideen am laufenden Band liefern, ne - die Ideen - was macht man damit - hm - das ist ja nicht so, daß sie sich jetzt so hinsetzen kann und denkt dann mal nach, und dann fällt ihr was ein oder auch nicht, sondern sie muß halt - ja, ich schreib mal: die Ideen, die ich entwickeln müßte, weil mir jetzt im Moment nichts Besseres einfällt.

English translation:

> ... well, she has to produce ideas non-stop ("Ideen am laufenden Band liefern") - ideas - what does one do with them - hm - you don't just sit there and think about something, and then you have an idea or you don't, but she has to sort of - well, yes, I'll write down "die Ideen, die ich entwickeln müßte" ("the ideas I would have to develop"), because I can't think of a better solution right now.

The student does not even recognize that she had actually found a very good translation ("Ideen am laufenden Band liefern"). She returns to a rather literal and unidiomatic rendering of "generate", with the excuse that she cannot think of anything else at the moment, a rather strange comment, if one considers the fact that she had produced a very fine translation a few moments ago.

This ambivalent attitude of our semi-professional translators was also observed by Séguinot(1989) in her case-study of a professional translator: "It appears that the translator first reaches an understanding of the meaning of the source text, puts the meaning which is retained into words as she is translating, and then returns to the expression level of the source text as memory fades" (p.36).

Fading of memory may be one of the psychological reasons for these processes. This would corroborate an observation made by Krings (1987) in his study of professional behaviour which he calls "Konzentrik" as opposed to "Linearität". Thus professionals seem to possess the skill of taking a larger amount of context into consideration than non-professionals. It can be assumed that short-term memory plays a certain part in this process.

But even if translators do remember their previous understanding of the text arrived at by paraphrasing, they will not make use of it as long as they do not regard paraphrases as proper translations. Paraphrases are not merely preliminary stages of translation. As teachers we should point out that they can indeed be just the version one is looking for.

The fact that students underrate paraphrases may stem from the idea that text analysis and translation are two distinctly separate phases and activities. This is obviously not the case. It could be seen from our protocols that the phase of understanding the source text is linked up with the phase of producing the translation via paraphrasing. There is thus a close interaction between analytic and productive activities. As far as meaning and comprehension are concerned, I believe that source text analysis and target-text recasting should not be taught as two distinctly separate phases. We should rather make it clear to our students that *in capturing, in their own words, the meaning of a text or passage they may have arrived at the most appropriate translation.*

1.4 Desirable attitudes: self-awareness and self-confidence

All of these explanations can be linked up again with the bottom-up and top-down processes I referred to in a number of instances. When paraphrasing, we take into account the larger context and often our knowledge of the world for our interpretation of the words in question, and we thus build our hypotheses through top-down processing. This reliance on world knowledge can be observed very well in the protocol just quoted in the utterance beginning with "das ist ja nicht so". Although top-down processing in the understanding of the text worked quite smoothly here, it seems that our students, nevertheless, did not have the courage to rely on these processes as much as they should have done, in other words, they lacked *self-confidence.*

The fact that the subjects automatically came up with quite adequate solutions that were subsequently lost could be observed not only in paraphrasing but also in the other problems discussed (fear of interferences, misuse of bilingual dictionaries). A knowledge of the solution-finding psycholinguistic processes may generally be helpful in preserving these solutions. And we could also see that a proper functioning of them may help avoid errors and mistranslations. Although these processes in normal communication do not take place on a cognitive level but are internalized and work more or less automatically, in translation becoming aware of them, if the need arises, will be part of the behaviour of the professional. Thus *self-awareness* seems to be one of the main features of professional translating (cf. Hönig 1991:88, Hönig 1993:89). We cannot expect, though, that translators will be aware of what they are doing at all critical moments. This would be unrealistic. What can we do if the psycholinguistic processes have not worked properly?

What always comes to light is the end product: the translation, often as a choice between variants. What translators then must have at their disposal are strategies for decision-making and for evaluating the end product, and these macro-strategies and micro-strategies, as Hönig calls them (1991:83ff., Hönig 1993, passim), can be taught and should be part of a translation training curriculum. Pragmatic and semantic text analysis, the proper use of dictionaries and translation quality assessment are certainly part of these strategies. These topics will be discussed in the following chapters.

As far as emotional factors are concerned, the subjects' insecurity and lack of courage observed when they were monitoring their search for solutions must eventually be replaced by *self-confidence*, which students will gain if we make them aware of the processes going on in their minds when they are translating, and also of the processes which should go on, so that, furnished with the macrostrategies mentioned, they will eventually possess the cognitive tools for professional work. The two psychological features which are part of the make-up of a professional translator, *self-awareness* and *self-confidence*, thus seem to be closely linked. It is through self-awareness that translators gain self-confidence (cf. Hönig 1991:88, Hönig 1993:89).

In a round table discussion I recently attended with professional translators one of the professionals maintained that translators very often had "weak personality structures". What he meant was that translators were not adventurous, dynamic, vigorous, in short not self-confident. In his opinion, the translating profession attracted such personalities. One reason for this may be that translating and interpreting are "serving" professions, and serving does not usually go together with a well developed ego (cf. Bühler 1993:97f.). This may be true, but we should at least consider another explanation. It may very well be that when our students embark on a translator training course, they are quite self-confident young people, but in the course of their studies they lose their self-confidence as a result of the criticism of their teachers.

When one looks at common teaching methods one sometimes gets the impression that students' self-confidence is undermined rather than strengthened (cf. Hönig 1988b:12). There is the "my-version-runs-as-follows" type of teacher, who listens to two or three students' translations and then, without much comment, reads out his own version. One of the reasons for this procedure seems to me that instructors very often have no clear idea about what they are doing. Königs in a survey he conducted among translation instructors in teacher training as well as translator training programs came to the conclusion that "the instructors in question had not given any thought whatsoever to the aims and purpose of a course in translation" (Königs 1979:116). Kiraly in this context talks of a "pedagogical gap" in translator training (Kiraly 1990:5).

Students, we cannot deny, very often feel confused when their translations are assessed and their mistakes are corrected, because their teachers do not reveal their criteria of evaluation. And if they do, they often restrict themselves to rules of grammar, while semantic, stylistic and pragmatic issues are decided on in a rather ad hoc manner or by the authority of the teacher's "feel for the language". Such subjective ways of judging are certainly of no great help to our students. They will not be able to learn something they can apply when they are faced with a problem next time.

The ability to discuss translations in an objective way is central to a translator's competence. Ideally, we should offer our students the chance to comment on their own translations in tests (cf. Holz-Mänttäri 1984:118f.). If numbers are small this should be possible. If translation classes and the number of candidates in examinations are too big, we will have to think of other possibilities. I have recently begun to offer seminars where students translate a text and comment on their solutions to translation problems. The texts and their translations are handed out to the participants some days before the seminar sessions so that everyone can read the translation critically. In the seminars the students then have to "defend" their work against critical comments from seminar members. The aim is that they learn to act as experts. Expert behaviour is not a personality trait, rather it is acquired role playing. Even "weakly structured" personalities can adopt expert professional roles. We may observe this in other walks of life. There is the doctor, a shy and reserved person in private life, but when talking to his patients he radiates confidence. There is the teacher, a quiet person privately, but when in front of his class he is dynamic, witty and inspiring. Charlie Chaplin, according to the women he lived with, was a rather boring person privately but on the screen he was one of the most fascinating comedians the world has ever seen.

How can we train expert role playing? We must provide our students with professional arguments. Statements such as "it sounds better", "I found it in the dictionary" are completely useless. Professionalism implies the ability to rationalize one's decision-making processes in an objective way, and the models offered by translation studies can provide the basis for acquiring this ability. In the subsequent chapters on text analysis, contrastive text linguistics, translation quality assessment and creative translation these methods will be presented.

They will help our students to increase both their self-awareness and self-confidence.

1.5 Error analysis revisited

When talking about error analysis at the beginning of this chapter I pointed out that it is rather speculative when it tries to explain the reasons of errors since it offers us no immediate observation of the translation process. However, in the light of the results gained from protocol-analysis some interpretations of errors may become more plausible. The examples of protocol-analyses presented so far have shown that there is often no proper balance between bottom-up and top-down processes, and that instead of correct understanding of a text what we get is misunderstanding. This can also be observed when analysing students' errors.

Firstly, it can happen that the meaning of a word stored in a student's memory is so dominant that it blots out the context completely. Secondly, it can also happen that the context is experienced in such a personal and dominating way, that it completely overshadows the meaning of a word that ought to have been activated. In both cases we can diagnose a predominance of top-down processes. In the first case it is the meaning already present in the student's memory, in the second case it is the expectation created by the preceding context, which makes it impossible for the student to recognize the meaning of the words in front of him or her, i.e. the bottom-up material. I shall illustrate what I mean. Here is an example of the first case.

In Margaret Mead's anthropological study *Male and Female* there is a description of the roles of men and women typical in American society around the time when the book was published in 1949. In a passage I used for translation, the notion of a "good wife" was described vividly and in great detail. The complementary notion of a "good husband" was mentioned but not described. A mistranslation resulted from the following sentence:

> (6)...both men and women share the same images of what makes a marriageable or an unmarriageable woman, a good husband, a fascinating lover whom any woman would be a fool to marry, or a born old bachelor. (Margaret Mead, *Male and Female*, Harmondsworth: Penguin Books 1962, S.271)

One of the students, a female, translated:

> ...einen faszinierenden Liebhaber, den jede Frau auf der Stelle heiraten würde...

which is, actually, the contrary of what was expressed in the original. Other female students translated the sentence in a similar way, e.g. "den jede Frau sofort heiraten würde". What had happened? There is a simple and often used explanation by teachers of translation which one might call the *carelessness hypothesis* which runs: The students did not concentrate sufficiently on the source text and did not read it closely enough.

This is a trivial and pedagogically rather useless explanation. Psycholinguistic analysis offers a much better one, which I propose to call the *hypothesis of misuse of top-down knowledge*. The somewhat stuffy idea behind the male and female roles in Margaret Mead's text, namely that a good lover cannot possibly be a good husband, is shaped by the historical situation the book refers to, the decades before the middle of the 20th century and possibly by Margaret Mead's own experience. The students who mistranslated the text may have read a meaning into it which was not there because they were preoccupied with their own idea of a fascinating lover shaped by their historical and cultural experience of the late twentieth century and maybe also by their personal wishes. For them, at least after the sexual revolution of the sixties, love, romance and sex were indispensable parts of marriage. Thus the comprehension process was dominated by top-down processes initiated by culturally based experiences, and bottom-up processes could not sufficiently take place. In other words, they found it hard to imagine the *scene* behind the text, because this scene did not fit in with the perhaps very vivid scenes in their minds.

I am aware of the fact that my way of explaining what went on in the students' minds is hypothetical, but from what we have seen in the protocols it seems likely, and one thing seems to be sure, namely that the *misuse-of-top-down-knowledge-hypothesis* has greater explanatory power than the carelessness-hypothesis.

The second case - the individual expectations created by the context are so overwhelming that they blot out the meaning of a word that ought to have been activated - can be illustrated by the following text specimen which deals with the travelling of young university graduates:

> (7) On the outback trail in Asia time is distorted. Young travellers, clothed in soiled cotton, spend hours waiting, resting on their propped back-packs filled with the barest of necessities: toiletries, a change of clothes, a sleeping bag, perhaps a tent, almost certainly a diary. Many of them, unused to Eastern food, will fall ill in cheap hotels...
>
> Graduates of many British and American Universities, and from many other parts of the world, are postponing entry into their national work-forces to venture overseas and experience the world at first hand. A survey of first-year graduates by the Career Services Office in Oxford shows that the number planning to travel and take temporary work abroad has increased significantly during the last five years...
>
> *(The Illustrated London News, Spring 1991)*

Line 9/10 *to venture overseas and experience the world at first hand* was translated by a student by "um ins Ausland zu reisen und zunächst einmal die Welt kennenzulernen". This makes sense within the context - we may have even have expected such a sentence - but it does not render the meaning of the English idiom *at first hand* which should have been translated here by "um die Welt aus erster Hand kennen zu lernen" or the like.

We may diagnose a deficiency in foreign language competence. The translator, obviously, did not know the idiomatic meaning of *at first hand* and thought that *at first* was here being used as a time adverb in the sense of "first of all". A native English speaker would not have made this error. What is interesting from a psycholinguistic point of view, however, is that this error has to some extent been motivated by the student's comprehension of the context which in turn led to faulty top-down processes. The topic of the preceding lines is indeed the "postponed" entry into professional life, and seen within this context the translation would indeed make sense. But within the larger context the way has been paved for the idiomatic meaning of at *first hand*. In the first lines of our text specimen there is a detailed description of these first hand experiences.

What is the pedagogical use of these psycholinguistic explanations? We need not confine ourselves to giving our students rather general advice such as: You ought to concentrate on the text! You ought to enlarge your knowledge of the foreign language! You must learn more idioms! We can show them in many cases how we can infer the meaning of words from the contexts in which they appear. If we make our students aware of the comprehension processes that go on in their minds we might be able to help them improve these processes. Processes which normally take place subconsciously can then become more controlled in the training phase.

This kind of training could take place in text analysis courses. The presentation of psycholinguistic models could be part of these courses. These models can help us to see that there is the text and its words and phrases (Fillmore's *frames*) which have a meaning potential, and there are the concepts, images, pictures, ideas etc. (Fillmore's *scenes*) in the mind of the reader and translator which are triggered off by the text. As teachers we must take care that there is a perfect balance between these two. When we observe that scenes do not fit frames, as in the examples just quoted, we can draw our students' attention to the actual text in front of them. For instance, in the text by Margaret Mead, we can show them how the ideas of the text were influenced by the historical situation which the book refers to and the time in which it was written. In other words, we can teach our students to see a text within its pragmatic context (cf. 3 on "Pragmatic analysis"). In the case of the text about travelling university graduates we can make our students aware of the structure of the text, of its line of thought. We can teach our students not only to see a word within its immediate but also within its larger context. There are linguistic models such as functional sentence perspective which can help us in this respect. This will be discussed in detail in Chapter 4 on "The analysis of meaning" and 5 "Text analysis and the use of dictionaries"). All this does not mean, however, that for professional translating the comprehension processes should remain conscious. In the same way as with grammatical rules, after some time of training and practice these processes may very well become internalized thus ensuring speedy and economical translation.

Chapter 2

Creativity in translation

2.1 Point of departure

In the first Chapter I made use of think-aloud protocols (TAPs) in order to find out where students have problems. In this chapter I am again using TAPs, but this time taking up a suggestion made by Lörscher (1992a:146) in order to find out where and how students are successful. Whereas my aim in the first Chapter was to find out what typically happened, I am now content to find out what occasionally happens. In other words, even if in ten pages of TAP transcriptions there is only one passage where creativity becomes visible, our data-based observations will have been worth while. My aim is to observe creative translation processes in order to use them as models for teaching.

Creative processes, as we shall see, are closely linked with successful processes. There are, of course, successful processes which do not require creativity (e.g. more or less automatized translation shifts and paraphrases, the use technical terms in standard situations) and which are routine for the experienced translator. I shall restrict myself to non-routine processes, because they are the ones which usually create problems and require creativity.

One might have thought that creativity would have been a popular topic in translation studies, but to my knowledge there have been no data-based studies in this area until now. There have, of course, been general discussions of creativity. Wilss (1988), for instance, in his book on cognition and translating, devotes a whole chapter to creativity and Alexieva (1990) examines creativity in simultaneous interpreting. The gist of their arguments seems to be very similar. Creative translation has to do with unpredictable non-institutionalised use of language (Wilss 1988:127) or the selection of a translation variant which is not rule-governed (Alexieva 1990:5). This is in line with the way creativity researchers define creativity by referring to the creative product. A creative product must be novel and must contain an element of surprise, it must be singular or at least unusual, but at the same time it must, of course, fulfil certain needs and fit in with reality (cf. Preiser 1976:2f.). Statements such as the ones by Wilss and Alexieva are certainly true, but they are nothing more than a starting point. The question we should try to answer is: How do we achieve these solutions?

In order to find out something about these types of translation process, I used texts with "poetic" features. These were not texts which could be labelled "literature" in the strict sense, but texts with a high degree of what Crystal and Davy call singularity (1969:76). I do not want to enter into a discussion of poetics and linguistics, but I think it is not unreasonable to expect that texts which deviate from general linguistic norms and set patterns and which in addition often have a very complex structure are especially suited for testing the translator's creativity (cf. Wilss 1988:112f.)

I used two texts of this type: an article from *Cosmopolitan* and a limerick by Edward Lear. 12 dialogue-protocols of these texts were analysed in 12 papers presented by students in seminars in 1989 and 1990, which I used as material for my observations. In addition, I made use of a dialogue-protocol of each of these texts produced in a seminar. The subjects, here again, were semi-professionals with a certain knowledge of translation strategies acquired in previous seminars. The texts to be translated had been analysed in class beforehand, so that their "poetic" quality should have been clear to the subjects.

If we want to talk about creativity in translation we must take into account the results produced by creativity research. I have only been able to scratch the surface, as it were, of the vast amount of research that has been done over the last few decades. Nevertheless, I shall venture to put forward a few ideas about possible links between models of creative thought and the translation process. I shall take the creative operations within Guilford's "Structure of Intellect Model" (Guilford 1975) as a starting point and try to apply them to the translation process.

2.2 Cognition and the four-phase model

Most psychologists use a four phase model of the creative process to get a clearer view of the complex activities going on in the human mind. These phases were first distinguished in 1913 by Poincaré who described them as *1. preparation 2. incubation 3. illumination 4. evaluation* (cf. Landau 1969:66f., Preiser 1976:42f., Ulmann 1968:21ff., Taylor 1975:16ff.) They will be referred to in the following sections when describing the mental processes which take place in creative translation.

In the preparatory phase cognition plays a major role. Problems are noticed and analysed, and relevant information and knowledge are accumulated. Some initial hypotheses may already have been formulated (Ulmann 1968:22f.). This phase seems to correspond to the stage of comprehension of the source text in the translation process, where text analysis and interpretation play a major role and where the function of the target text is being established. The psycholinguistic models of bottom-up and top-down processes and frames-and-scenes can be used at this stage in order to make students aware of their comprehension processes.

It has been argued that translators are tied down by the source text in their creation of the target text and that their work is re-creative rather than creative (cf. Wilss 1988:111). Of course, translators are not as free in their productions as writers are, but in the first phase of the creative process they must have the same ability to recognize a problem, gather relevant information and form initial hypotheses about possible solutions as any creative person.

It is obvious that the preparatory phase involves conscious mental activities, that an awareness of purpose is important here. It will be seen that cognition not only plays an important part in the preparatory phase but also in the evaluative phase. We shall see that the four phases are, in fact, only a construct, and that these phases are actually often simultaneous.

We usually associate creativity with production. Thus within the field of language, saying things, writing and translating texts are typical creative activities. But what about comprehension? Is there not something like creative comprehension? We sometimes even talk of creative miscomprehension. It is a commonplace that when rereading a text after some time we understand it in a different way. When we read Shakespeare's great tragedies as adolescents and when we read them again after twenty or thirty years we certainly arrive at different interpretations of these plays. Comprehension, as we have seen now in many instances, is not only guided by what we hear or read but also by our personal knowledge and experience. Understanding is not merely a receptive but also a productive process. Thus rereading a text, especially after some time has passed, may lead us to new insights, to a novel way of seeing it, and these interpretations may well be called creative. It follows that when translating works of art creative understanding is part of the process. One might try to apply Guilford's notion of *divergent thinking*, which I shall deal with below, to the comprehension process, and it would be interesting to see if these things can be observed in think-aloud protocols. For this purpose, however, one should perhaps use "more demanding" literary texts than the ones I have used so far. So at present, when observing creativity I have restricted myself to the reverbalization phase.

2.3 Fluency of thinking

Probably the most basic quality needed for creative activity is an ability which Guilford calls "fluency". It helps to produce a large number of thoughts, associations or ideas for a given problem in a short space of time (Guilford 1975:40) and plays an important part during the *incubation phase*. Does fluency play a role in the translation process and what form does it take?

One of our sample texts dealt with the kind of situation which leads to too much drinking. It was vividly described as follows:

> How well the summer wine goes down, whilst you bask in the balm of an island evening, fanned by the flattery of murmuring machos and lulled by the lilt of gypsy guitars.
> (*Cosmopolitan*, August 1980:82)

This text specimen is marked by a number of features which should be preserved in the translation in order to create the scenic effect. There is alliteration (*bask, balm, fanned, flattery* etc.), there are metaphors (*bask in the balm, fanned by the flattery*), and there is also a regular (dactylic) rhythm in the last part of the sentence.

The subjects were concerned with the translation of *murmuring machos*:

> A: ...umschmeichelt von den...also Casanova war schon
>   mal nicht schlecht. Jetzt müssen wir nur noch die Verbindung herstellen. Kühner Casanovas...
> B: kühner, kerniger und ortskundiger Casanovas (Lachen)
> A: k, was gibt es denn mit k?
> B: Küche, Kleiderschrank, Kinder (Lachen)
> A: Kinderreicher Casanovas (Lachen).Kerniger Casanovas.
> B: Nee. (Pause) Liebestoller Latin Lovers.
> A: Ja!

English translation:

> A: "umschmeichelt von den... Casanovas" ("caressed by the...Casanova") wasn't bad, to begin with. Now we must find an adjective. "Kühner Casanovas..."
> B: "kühner, kerniger und ortskundiger Casanovas" ("bold, robust Casanovas who know the place") (laughter)
> A: k, what can we find with a k?
> B: "Küche, Kleiderschrank, Kinder" ("kitchen, wardrobe, children") (laughter)
> A: "Kinderreicher Casanovas" ("Casanovas with many children") (laughter) "kerniger Casanovas"
> B: No. (Pause) "Liebestoller Latin Lovers" ("love-crazed Latin lovers").
> A: Yes, great!

Fluency manifests itself here in the production of quite a number of adjectives which produce alliteration. It is interesting to note that form is predominant over meaning in the beginning, which is a typical feature of word fluency tests as developed by psychologists (cf. Ulmann 1968, 79). In fact, when judged by their meaning the words are quite absurd. When thinking has become fluent, semantic considerations seem to set in, which then lead to the semantically and formally adequate solution "liebestoller Latin Lovers", which also preserves a regular rhythm, although not the dactylic one.

In order to train fluency the technique of *brainstorming* has been developed, where in the "green-light stage" all kinds of associations are encouraged and judgement is deferred. It can to some extent be linked to the incubation phase (cf. Osborn 1953:72, Preiser 1976:96; Clark 1966:54ff.). A typical feature of this phase seems to be both physical and psychological relaxation. It has been observed that new ideas even appear while dreaming (Preiser 1976:45; Ulmann 1968:24ff.). This relaxation seems to be very important for the creative translation process as well.

It could be observed in the protocols, and it is also a common experience, that when trying hard to find a solution to a problem our minds are sometimes blocked, and "illumination" is thus impeded. We all know the situation when we try in vain to recall a person's name and after a short time, during which we have been engaged with some other task, we all of a sudden remember it. This technique of leaving one's mind alone for a while and thus creating the necessary relaxation, which I propose to call *parallel-activity technique* was also made use of by the students I observed.

In a number of instances the subjects interrupted the translation process by going to the kitchen to get a bar of chocolate or a drink, by going to the toilet, by putting a new cassette into the tape-recorder etc., and when they returned to their task they suddenly produced a bright idea. It was observed that even blowing one's nose could have this effect.

In the text quoted above on too much drinking the subjects were again engaged in translating "fanned by the flattery of murmuring machos":

...

A: "Mandeläugige Männer" hätte ich gesagt, oder so, das...

B: Ach so, zwei "m"s.

A: Normalerweise sagt man "mandeläugige Mädchen".

B: Ja. (7 Sekunden Pause) Laß dich doch mal von diesen schönen Spanienbildern da an der Wand inspirieren (lacht).

A: Da sind keine Männer drauf (lacht, 5 SekundenPause).

B: Ja, irgendwas "lulled by the lilt of gypsy guitars".

(Die Kasette wird umgedreht, ca. 10 Sekunden Pause)

A: Jetzt habe ich eben gesagt "umschmeichelt von bewundernden Blicken".

B: Ja, das klingt doch!

A: Dann lassen wir das mit den Männern doch ganz weg.

B: Ja.

A: Also sind aus den "murmuring machos" "bewundernde Blicke" geworden (lacht)

English translation:

A: "Mandeläugige Männer" ("almond-eyed men") I would have said, something

like that...
B: I see, two "m"s.
A: Normally, the phrase is "mandeläugige Mädchen" ("almond-eyed girls").
B: True. (Pause of 7 seconds) Why don't you let yourself be inspired by those beautiful pictures of Spain on the wall over there? (laughs)
A: There aren't any men in these pictures (pause of 5 seconds)
B: Well, something "lulled by the lilt of gypsy guitars".
(Pause of 10 seconds while the cassette is turned over)
A: Now I just said "umschmeichelt von bewundernden Blicken" ("caressed by admiring looks").
B: Yes, great!
A: Then we'll leave the men out, shall we?
B: Yes.
A: So the "murmuring machos" have turned into "bewundernde Blicke" ("admiring looks") (laughs).

Before the turning over of the cassette the search for a solution seems to have got stuck. With "Mädchen" (1.3) the subjects had got on the wrong track, and the pause seems to indicate some mental block. Then after the casette is turned over, subject A comes up with a new suggestion (l. 9 and 14/15), which is the result of having moved away from the previous pattern and having shifted the phrase of the source text, a typical feature of the creative process which I shall deal with in a moment.

It seems to me that during these kinds of activities the translator's consciousness is diverted from the immediate task, and he or she does not feel compelled to find a solution. At a conscious level the mind is at rest, but at the same time mental activity goes on subconsciously.

2.4 Divergent thinking

According to Guilford *divergent production*, which is typically related to the incubation and illumination phase, contrasts with *convergent production*:

> ...divergent production is a broad search, usually in an open problem, in which there are a number of possible answers. I also sometimes say that it is a generation of logical alternatives. Fluency of thinking is the name of the game. Convergent production, on the other hand, is a focused search, for, from the nature of the given information or problem, one particular answer is required. I sometimes say that it is the generation of logical imperatives. (Guilford 1975:40)

I mentioned above that divergent thinking may play a part in text analysis. In my TAPs there are no instances of this, maybe because text analysis took place in class before the texts were actually translated. Also, the texts were perhaps too simple to offer real problems of interpretation. Nevertheless divergent thinking in text analysis may be an aspect worth studying. We know that in the interpretation of literary works alternative approaches often produce novel insights. For instance, when we look at the history of studies on Franz Kafka there is the biographical, the religious, the philosophical and the aesthetic approach, all of which reveal aspects of his work that have not been seen so clearly before.

In the protocol-passages just quoted, the process of solution finding, which in these cases can be related to the the illumination phase, could not be directly observed because it went on during a pause. The results, however, show that divergent thinking must have taken place. By the use of convergent thinking the subjects would never have arrived at "umschmeichelt von bewundernden Blicken" for "fanned by the flattery of murmuring machos" but would have tried to find an equivalent word for "machos" on the basis of the feature HUMAN BEING which, in fact, they did, although in vain, before the creative pause. It was only through divergent thinking that they could free themselves from the idea that a word denoting a human being should be translated by a word of the same semantic category. What the translators performed here is a typical "shift", a well known procedure in translation studies, which means that we move away from the linguistic form of the source text and recreate the meaning or function of the form by a different linguistic form in the target text. Shifting as a basic translating activity thus, among other things, seems to be closely related with creative behaviour.

Another important feature observed by Gestalt psychologists and associated with the incubation process is the restructuring and reorganization of facts (cf. Ulmann 1968:27ff.), an activity which comes very close to what Guilford calls *transformation* (cf. also de Bono's "lateral thinking" 1970), and which seems to me, basically, a specification of divergent thinking:

> The chief role of transformations in our creative thinking is that they provide needed flexibility. How often do we persist in trying to solve the wrong problem? There is no headway until our conception of the problem is revised. How often do we persist in trying to use an old solution because it worked before but will not work under even slightly altered conditions? Sometimes a very simple transformation is the key to an important invention, as when the eye of a needle was moved from the blunt end where it had always been to the sharp end where it is needed in the sewing machine. (Guilford 1975:44).

This type of mental process could also be observed in the protocols. Two subjects were trying to translate the first two lines of a limerick by Edward Lear:

There was an Old Man of Nepaul,
From his horse had a terrible fall;
But, though split quite in two,
By some very strong glue,
They mended that man of Nepaul.
(Ernest Rhys (ed.), *A Book of Nonsense*, London: Dent 1970:29)

The subjects began translating by looking for rhyming words. They started off with "Pferd" for "horse" in the second line, but could not find a rhyming town-name. Then they tried a different procedure:

A: Man könnte natürlich auch "Fall" nehmen und eine Stadt auf "Fall"
    finden
B: oder "Sturz"
A: oder "hernieder, vom Pferd hernieder"
B: wie Stadt - Land - Fluß
A: statt Pferd ja auch "Mähre"
B: auf "Mähre" bestimmt ein schwedischer Städtename
A: schreiben wir mal auf: Mähre, Gaul, Pferd, Stute,
Esel, fiel herunter, fiel hernieder, Pony.
B: Jetzt haben wir schon mal acht Begriffe
A: "Pferd" ist schwer.
B: auf "Stute"
A: "Esel"
B: ja "Esel"
A: Wesel
B: ja gut!
A: Ein alter Mann aus Wesel, der fiel von seinem Esel.

English translation:

A: We could use "Fall" and look for a town rhyming with "Fall"
B: or "Sturz" (synonym for "Fall")
A: or "hernieder, vom Pferd hernieder" ("down from his horse")
B: like that game "Stadt-Land-Fluß"
A: instead of "Pferd" we can also say "Mähre"
B: and for "Mähre" there must be a Swedish town-name
A: Let's write down what we have have got: "Mähre,Gaul, Pferd, Stute, Esel, fiel
    herunter, fiel hernieder, Pony."
B: Now we have got eight words, not bad.
A: "Pferd" is difficult.
B: rhyming with "Stute"
A: "Esel"
B: yes, "Esel"
A: "Wesel"

B: yes, splendid!
A: "Ein alter Mann aus Wesel, der fiel von seinem Esel".

Here we have a good example of changing the strategy as a manifestation of divergent thinking and transformation. At first the subjects tried to find synonyms for "Fall" as a basis for a rhyming town-name. Then, suddenly, they tried a different technique by looking for words which are semantically related with "Pferd", in addition to synonyms for "Fall, fallen" (ll.6ff.). In a way, two conceptions of the problem, or rather, two ways of solving the problem, were competing with each other. Changing the strategy is accompanied here by fluency in that the subjects quickly produced quite a large number of synonyms. I shall not discuss the metre of the lines they found, which does not render the dactyls of the original, but I think the translation is successful as far as rhyme and semantics are concerned, and the solution has indeed been achieved by a certain amount of reorganisation of the relevant facts.

It may also be important to note that the subjects did not explicitly state the principle of their search. They did not say: "Let's use a semantic method and look for synonyms for "horse!" It seems as if the principle had been hovering in the air all the time and the subjects finally got hold of it. The mental process appears to have been subconscious to some extent, as indeed could be expected during the incubation phase. ✓✓

Divergent thinking and transformations are, of course, no novel phenomena. They have always occurred in the translation process, but perhaps we have not been fully aware of them, or have not been able to categorise them with sufficient precision until now. Hönig provides an excellent example of what is to me divergent thinking under the heading "interplay between cognition and intuition" (1990:153f.). He asked a group of seven semi-professionals (i.e. advanced students) to translate an advertisement by British banks, which by the use of a parable describes the dangers which a naive investor needs to be aware of. The "hero" of the parable is a honey-bee trying to gather honey from the attractive offers:

> Perched on a branch high above the flower beds, he mocked their giant hollyhocks, scorned their cornflowers, chuckled at their honeysuckle.

The subjects realized that assonances were important for the effect of the text, and after some time one of them suggested the translation:

> ...behandelte die Stiefmütterchen stiefmütterlich...., ließ die Lilien links liegen.

What remained to be done was to find a third collocation using the same pattern, which posed some difficulties. One of the subjects described his solution-searching strategy: "I look for verbs expressing disdain, and then I try to find names for flowers or plants that form assonances with these verbs." After some further futile attempts another student in the group suggested that one should start off with the other member of the assonance, with the name of a flower or plant. After a short while the students were successful. One of them mentioned "Flieder", and another one spontaneously produced:

"Und den Flieder - mied er".

This, I think, is a very good example of what Guilford calls "generation of logical alternatives" (1975:40).The students did not persist in using one strategy throughout, but used the alternative one that offered itself. Hönig makes a point in saying that the change of strategy here was a conscious, i.e. cognitive, process. As we have seen in the translation of the limerick, strategies need not be raised to consciousness. The main thing is that divergent thinking takes place, consciously or subconsciously. When we teach, however, it will be helpful to draw our students' attention to the ways and methods divergent thinking can get started.

2.5 Emotions

When Guilford talks of "Structure of Intellect" he does not refer to emotions. The creative process, however, as most mental activities, is not only governed by intellect but also by emotion. Some neurologists have put forward the hypothesis that creative thinking is closely connected with the anterior hypothalamus in the brain, which is the centre of libido and lust and motivates not only sexual fantasies but fantasies and daydreaming of all types. Such fantasies seem to be important for creative thinking. Thus, sexual desire appears to be closely connected with creativity, and one of the conditions for creative work seems to be an atmosphere of approval and sympathetic encouragement (Stanley-Jones 1970:154f.)

It could be observed in the protocols, especially during incubation, when relaxation was part of the game, that a certain amount of laughter and fooling around took place amongst the subjects if they did not find their solutions at once. This, in combination with the "parallel-activity technique" described above, also prevented them from being stuck up a blind alley, and promoted new ideas. Laughter can also be a sign of sympathetic approval on the part of a subject and may help to create the gratification-oriented condition postulated by neurologists.

According to psychologists we also find strong emotions at the illumination stage of the creative process which have even been compared by neurologists to coital furor (Stanley-Jones 1970, 157). Emotions can be observed in our protocols in the comments and reactions to solutions. Although intonation and tone of voice, which for technical reasons could not be transcribed, would tell us more about this aspect, the actual words used do indeed show positive feelings. We have "ja gut" as a reaction to the solution in the limerick (1.17) and "ja, das klingt doch" as a reaction to "bewundernde Blicke" in the protocol about the Holiday Hangover text (protocol, 1.13).

2.6 Evaluation

The four-phase model is a theoretical construct, which helps us to isolate specific features of the creative process, rather than a realistic image of reality. We thus cannot draw a clear line between preparation, incubation, illumination and evaluation. This is confirmed by the protocols, and it becomes evident that some models need to be modified when we want to apply them to the translation process. In translation, brainstorming, for instance, does not seem to be clearly divided up into a green-light and a red-light stage. We can observe phases where there is a large amount of productivity, where ideas stimulate new ideas and where at the same time constructive criticism leads to their improvement. Can this still be called incubation or must it be called illumination or even evaluation? As to emotions during this phase, do they suggest that there is a positive evaluation of the idea that has come to mind? But then what about the evaluation stage that is supposed to follow rather than accompany illumination?

Preiser (1972:48) has drawn attention to the fact that the phases do not normally simply follow each other in a sequence, but there are moves backward and forward, in loops as it were, and some phases are gone through repeatedly. If this is true, we may suppose that there is a close interrelation between production and reflection, which would mean that we can only look for ideas when we have become fully aware of the problem, and we cannot accept ideas unless we have evaluated them according to their appropriateness.

Thus illumination appears to be closely connected with evaluation, and Ulmann, in fact, treats both phases in the same chapter (Ulmann 1968, 29ff.). There are numerous instances in the protocols where it becomes obvious that lack of evaluation during incubation and illumination leads to a loss of good ideas. Quite often the subjects produced appropriate and highly original translations which nevertheless did not appear in the final version of their target text. In the article quoted above about holiday hangovers, there was a passage about the after-effects of too much drinking:

How different the next day when your head is hurtling
like an off-course cable car and the sun slugs you right in the eye.
(*Cosmopolitan*, August 1980, 82)

The relevant passage in the protocol reads:

A: ...dann muß der letzte Satz aber noch besser werden!
Wie ernüchternd ist dagegen der Morgen danach. Die Lichtstrahlen schmerzen wie hunderttausend Nadelstiche. Gibt es nicht irgendwie sowas? Da gibt es etwas, aber ich komme nicht drauf.
(Pause)
B: Ein Brummschädel zum Platzen - so etwas vielleicht.

English translation:

A: ..but the last sentence must be improved. "Wie ernüchternd ist dagegen der Morgen danach. Die Lichtstrahlen schmerzen wie hunderttausend Nadelstiche" ("How sobering the morning after. The sunbeams hurt like the pricks of a hundred thousand needles.") Isn't there something like that? There must be something, but I can't think of it now.
(pause)
B:"Ein Brummschädel zum Platzen"("a buzzing head as if it's going to split") - maybe something like that.

After a lengthy discussion the subjects settled for:

Der Schädel brummt und man erleidet Höllenqualen. Grelles Licht und Lärm werden einfach unerträglich. ("You've got a buzzing head and are suffering the torments of hell. Bright light and noise are simply unbearable")

They did not seem to have noticed that they had found a much more adequate phrase right at the beginning ("die Licht-strahlen schmerzen wie hunderttausend Nadelstiche"). One might argue, as Toury (1991) does, that there is a difference between written and spoken translation and that, as a consequence, translations that are spoken, as in the TAPs, are not necessarily regarded as proper translations (Toury 1988:60f.). Our subjects, certainly, did not regard their dialogue as part of the final translation. Another reason seems to me that they did not recognize the highly metaphorical quality of the sentence in the source text and thus cast aside their first quite adequate translation. This example clearly illustrates the necessity of a close interrelation of the various phases. The result of the preparatory phase, if it had been achieved at all - a recognition of the metaphorical quality of the passage - was apparently no longer present during the illumination stage where it should have become the criterion for evaluating the creative product.

2.7 Teaching creative translation

My empirical investigations were carried out with a view to improving the teaching of translation. Are there didactic consequences that can be drawn from the observations? The most obvious conclusion is that we must take care our students always preserve a critical and evaluative attitude toward the ideas that come to their minds. This observation is in line with the need for *self-awareness* suggested in Chapter 1. At every moment of the incubation and illumination phase, translators must be able to step back, as it were, and observe what they have been doing. More specifically, this means that they should always be able to call to mind the results of their text analysis and the results of their consideration of the function of a passage within a text in a given situation in a given culture. In other words, microstrategies should always be governed by macrostrategies (cf. Hönig 1991). This is the basic requirement. There are also a number of other, more specific conditions favourable to creative thought.

If psychologists are correct in saying that creative thought is gratification-oriented, then students should be able to take a positive attitude toward their task. They should like their text (and maybe their teacher) or at least should like translating it. The problem must not appear too big for them, nor too simple either. As teachers, we should take care to select texts with an appropriate degree of difficulty for the specific stage of translator training.

When a text is being translated in class, criticism should never be harsh. We should try to create *that atmosphere of sympathetic encouragement* which, according to psychological research, seems to be so conducive to creative thought.

At the end of the first Chapter, it will be remembered, I pointed out that *self-confidence* was one of our main psychological teaching goals. The emotions favourable for creative thought suggest that self-confidence is also one of the prerequisites for creative translation.

If creative thinking gets stuck, we should use techniques for removing the mental block. We might systematically use the *parallel-activity technique* observed in the protocols, by the use of which the subjects unintentionally diverted their attention from the task in front of them and thus created the relaxation necessary for removing the blockage. Students will have to find their own individual methods here. It may be going to the fridge for one person or a walk round the block for another. It would be helpful to find out the ideal time-span of diversion.

It has been suggested by psychologists, and it could also be observed in the protocols, that *fluency* and *divergent thinking* are the main mental abilities necessary for creative thought. Can these abilities be trained? Is there something like translational fluency? The ability to find synonyms or semantically related words for a given expression seems to be a basic requirement for creative translation. We shall have to find methods of training and improving this ability.

Translational flexibility or the ability to perform *transformations*, which is based on divergent thinking, was observed in one of the protocols quoted above as the skill of changing the technique of searching for a solution. We saw that this flexibility had as its prerequisite the ability *of abstracting meaning from its linguistic form.* This seems to be the most basic requirement for a translator, and linguistic and psycholinguistic methods could be used in order to make our students aware of this process.

Cognitive semantics may be helpful in this respect. In the examples quoted, it is interesting to note that the subjects put things together into categories which according to the structuralist theory of semantic fields do not form categories at all. Thus "Pferd" with its semantically related words was joined together with "Fall", and "Machos" with "bewundernden Blicken". In the case of "Machos" and "Latin Lovers", however, it could be argued that there are indeed common semantic features which can be interpreted culturally.

It might be a step in the right direction if we made students aware of how these mental categories come into being. Here again, the *scenes and frames model* may be of explanatory use. *Prototype and cognitive semantics* may also offer some explanations. It has been observed that we put things which are in the same domain of experience together into categories via *chaining* (cf. Lakoff 1987:91ff.), and it could be argued that in the limerick by Edward Lear the text itself formed the *experiential domain* on the basis of which concepts were joined together. And in the text about holiday hangovers the line "fanned by the flattery of murmuring machos" might be seen to be linked up with "bewundernden Blicken" by an experiential domain which can be described as "men's positive evaluation of a woman's physical appearance". The principle of chaining, described by Lakoff (1987:91ff.), by which categories are structured and enlarged, seems, in fact, to be very similar to Guilford's divergent thinking. It would seem then that the basic principles of human cognition are similar to creative thought, which would mean that creativity is not a gift of the select few but a basic feature of the human mind and that we can all be creative when we translate. It has been suggested by Snell-Hornby (1988) that prototype and gestalt semantics should form the methodological basis for translation studies. When it comes to explaining creative translation-processes she may very well be right.

It might be argued that fluency and flexibility are a result of teamwork. In the protocols, there were always two subjects who searched for solutions. Undoubtedly, a stimulus from outside can be very helpful for both fluency and flexibility. But then, could not the processes that led up to the creative results also take place within one mind? We can, and in our minds we often do, talk to ourselves, and the dialogues that take place between two people might in a similar way take place within one person. Therefore, in order to improve one's fluency and flexibility each individual should know that these mental processes exist and how they function.

Can we train creativity? It may be possible to train fluency and divergent thinking by other than linguistic tasks. In this matter we shall have to ask the advice of psychologists who have developed test batteries for creativity which might also be used for training purposes (see Ulmann 1968:78ff.).

I have talked about teaching creative translation. These are ambitious aims. I think we shall have achieved something if we only make our students aware of what is going on in their minds during the creative process (cf.Guilford 1975:52). An awareness of the features of creativity may at least help them direct their own mental activities to some extent. Here again, not only *self-confidence* but also *self-awareness* seems to be one of the typical features of successful translating.

Chapter 3

Pragmatic analysis

3.0 Overview

The terms *pragmatic* and *pragmatics* have a special sense in linguistics and translation studies. *Pragmatics* is the study of the relationship between an utterance or text and its user, i.e. its speaker/writer and its hearer/reader. Language users do not exist in a vacuum, but operate in specific situations. When analysing linguistic events such as translations, we therefore need to take into account the relationship between situation, language user and text, and this is considered in section 3.1. When making utterances or writing texts, language users usually do not do so without any purpose. Rather they have an intention, which may sometimes be different from the actual meaning of the words used. The relationship between utterances or texts and the writer's intention will be discussed in section 3.2. The things we say, imply or allude to are not only determined by situation and by our intentions, but also by the culture we live in, a topic to be discussed in section 3.3. The influence of situation and culture on what we say or write may sometimes be so strong that they determine the form of texts. Certain linguistic features of texts may become conventionalized, a phenomenon which is referred to in linguistics as text type conventions and which will be dealt with in sections 3.4 and 3.5. The chapter is rounded off with some considerations of the didactic implications of the pragmatic approach (section 3.6).

3.1 Situational dimensions

Interferences can produce howlers. This happens not only with students, as we have seen in the last chapter, but also with professional translators. In the preface to his well-known autobiography A.S. Neill writes about the beginnings of Summerhill:

> Years ago, in one of my books, I wrote that when interviewing a prospective teacher, my test was: "What would you do if a child called you a bloody fool?" It is my test today, except that bloody - never a real swear word outside British realms - has been changed to a more popular expletive.
> (A.S. Neill, *Orange Peel Neill*, New York 1972)

The question Neill put as a test was translated into German as:

> Was würden Sie tun, wenn ein Kind Sie einen blutigen Narr nennt?
> (A.S. Neill, *Birnenstiel Neill*, übersetzt von Monika Kulow und Harry Rowohlt, Reinbeck bei Hamburg 1982)

Faced with this translation the prospective teacher's answer to this question ought to have been: "I would try to improve the child's linguistic competence."

The translators' mistake can be explained. It may have been caused by the formal similarity between English "bloody" and German "blutig". "Bloody" is a false friend of the "untrustworthy" type who are sometimes good friends but not always. One of its meanings *(covered with blood)* can indeed be translated by "blutig", but in our sentence "bloody" has a different meaning which in the *Dictionary of Contemporary English* (DCE) is described as

> *esp. BrE infml, not polite* **1** (used for giving force to an expression or judgement): *Don't be such a bloody fool! | It's bloody marvellous! | Bloody hell!* " **2** (used as an almost meaningless addition to angry speech): *I got my bloody foot caught in the bloody chair, didn't I? | "Will you lend me L 10?" "Not bloody likely!"* (= certainly not!)

To pick out the meaning of a polysemous word which fits into the context is certainly the first step to a good translation. The next step would be finding an adequate equivalent. This proves to be difficult here because "bloody", as the DCE tells us, is "almost meaningless". Linguistically speaking it has no referential or denotative meaning. But it has connotative, social or *pragmatic* meaning, in the sense that its "meaning" is constituted by the relation between the word and its users, and it may thus serve as a good example to demonstrate the use of pragmatic analysis.

To begin with, the DCE-entry contains the labels *BrE, infml, not polite.* These labels refer to the *situation* in which the word is used. More specifically, *BrE* refers to the national origin of the speaker. "Bloody" is typically British usage, Americans would use "the more popular expletive" alluded to by Neill. The labels *infml, not polite* refer to the degree of intimacy and possibly also to the status relationship between speaker and hearer. "Bloody" is used when there is a certain degree of closeness and maybe also social equality between speaker and hearer where some conventionalized forms of politeness are not obligatory. In our example the pupil talks to his teacher as if he were one of his classmates.

Situational analysis has been one of the topics of translation studies for some time. Let us deal with it for a moment in order to provide the necessary theoretical background for the analysis of our translation problem. Situational analysis rests on the idea that non-linguistic situational factors are reflected in linguistic forms. House (1977:37ff.) uses Crystal/Davy's (1969:64ff.) model of situational constraints with some minor modifications as a standard for translation quality assessment, and this model has also been adopted by Hönig/Kussmaul (1981:65ff.). More recently Hatim/Mason (1990:36ff.) have made use of Halliday/McIntosh/ Strevens'(1964) model which actually forms part of the basis for Crystal/Davy. I shall make use of House's model which to me seems more specific than Halliday/McIntosh/Strevens and which has also stood the test of application to translation quality assessment. The situational dimensions which are reflected in language-use are according to House(1977:42ff.):

Dimensions of Language User:

1. GEOGRAPHICAL ORIGIN
2. SOCIAL CLASS
3. TIME

Dimensions of Language Use:

1. MEDIUM
2. PARTICIPATION
3. SOCIAL ROLE RELATIONSHIP
4. SOCIAL ATTITUDE
5. PROVINCE

GEOGRAPHICAL ORIGIN is used not only to refer to regional dialects but also to national varieties of English, such as British English, American English, Australian English, Indian English etc. In our example this dimension is relevant; it is, in fact, topicalized by Neill:"...never a real swearword outside British realms".

The dimension SOCIAL CLASS is used to refer to class or social dialect, such as Cockney in English. *Bleeding* or *bleedn',* one might say, is more working class than *bloody*. "TIME refers to those features of a text which provide clues to a text's temporal provenance" (House 1977:40). A sixteenth century counterpart to "bloody fool" might be "prating knave". MEDIUM refers to the written spoken division. PARTICIPATION is used to distinguish between monologue and dialogue. Tag-questions, for instance, are typical of a text with dialogue character. The child's utterance quoted in our text would become part of a dialogue if it ran: "You are a bloody fool, aren't you?" In addition, the contraction "aren't" would be a sign of the spoken medium.

In my experience, SOCIAL ROLE RELATIONSHIP and SOCIAL ATTITUDE are the dimensions which can be observed most frequently. SOCIAL ROLE RELATIONSHIP can be of three types: equal-to-equal, as in our example, lower-to-higher and higher-to-lower. If the relationship between speaker and hearer in Neill's example had been lower to higher, which would have been the traditional relationship between pupil and teacher, an utterance such as "bloody fool" would not have been possible. Showing anger and disrespect would definitely have been a sign of bad behaviour. A typical form of address would have been "Sir" or "Miss". If the roles had been higher to lower - the traditional relationship between teacher and pupil - the form of address used by a teacher for his/her pupils in the days Neill refers to would probably have been the surname; nowadays it would be the Christian name.

House makes a point in distinguishing between relatively permanent positional roles (e.g. of teacher, priest, etc.) and relatively transient situational roles (e.g. of guest, visitor in prison etc.) (House 1976:45). I find it difficult to apply these categories to our example. Pupil and teacher, one would have thought, are positional roles with unequal status. But then in Summerhill there is social equality between pupils and teachers. Do we have to talk of positions or situations here? Do we have situational roles within school and positional roles outside school? But what if Summerhill pupils meet Summerhill teachers outside school. The main point seems to me that we should talk of roles. We do not need any further specifications. Roles are adapted to situations, and this is what, in fact, always happens in human communication. Our lives seem to be strings of situational role-playing. The big boss of a firm will exercise his position of authority when signing a contract or when making decisions; he will be well advised, however, to exercise solidarity when discussing problems with colleagues or the works committee, and when asking his secretary if she could do overtime and type an urgent report, he will most certainly act from a lower to higher position. Furthermore, as was suggested to me by Hans Vermeer, communicative roles can be accepted or rejected by people, and there are assumptions about the roles played by the communicative partner. A teacher may play the role of class-mate, but his pupils may think that he should stick to his role of teacher. A pupil may assume that the teacher acts as his playmate, but the teacher may still keep up his role as teacher.

SOCIAL ATTITUDE refers to the various degrees of social distance or proximity. Talk between classmates, between friends, within the family is marked by closeness or very little social distance. Conversation between strangers, on the other hand, is marked by a higher degree of social distance. Forms of address are especially sensitive to these dimensions. "Close" forms are Christian names, pet names and forms like "dear", "darling", "honey" etc. "Distant" forms are "sir", "madam", "ladies and gentlemen", titles etc. It may very well be that one and the same form, such as "darling" or "sir" indicates both SOCIAL ROLE RELATIONSHIP and SOCIAL ATTITUDE. Nevertheless, these dimensions have distinctive force. For instance, both addressing someone by "sir"/"madam" and addressing someone by his/her surname are forms indicating the ATTITUDE of social distance, but "sir"/"madam" are also signs of lower to higher SOCIAL ROLE RELATIONSHIP, whereas addressing someone by his/her surname is not. Here again, there are assumptions about roles, and roles may be accepted or rejected. Having known a person for some time we may start calling him by his Christian name, assuming that there is sufficient social proximity to warrant this behaviour, but the other person may react in a cool manner and stick to surnames.

PROVINCE according to House is a very wide category. It reflects "the area of operation of the language activity" (House 1976:48) or, to use Crystal/Davy's definition, "the occupational or professional activity being engaged in" (Crystal/Davy 1969:71). It is thus a very important dimension for professional translation. It is a category which takes account of the fact that there are specific occupational or professional languages such as "legal language", "language of technology", "medical language", all of which have their own special vocabulary and/or terminology.

House does not distinguish between PROVINCE and MODALITY as Crystal/Davy do. MODALITY refers to further linguistic specifications within a given province. Thus within the language of technology we have instruction manuals, technical reports, advertising brochures, patent specifications etc. MODALITY, in fact, refers to a linguistic category which has proved to be extremely important for the teaching of professional translation. I am referring to what is called *Textsorte* in German and for want of a better term is usually translated as *text type* into English. Names of text types are for instance "business letter", "instruction manual", "textbook", "scholarly monograph", "lecture", "sermon" etc. It has been observed that these text types have specific linguistic conventions, and a translator has to know these conventions in order to produce translations which will be taken seriously by their professional readers. Therefore the dimension of MODALITY should not be dropped. I shall discuss text types and their conventions later in this chapter.

When talking about these things in non-technical English we sometimes use phrases like "switching register", and one might prefer to use the word *register* to refer to these situational conditions. In linguistic terminology, however, the term *register* has been used much more comprehensively by Halliday/McIntosh/Strevens for whom the term includes subject matter of discourse, the spoken or written mode and the relation of participants (Halliday/McIntosh/Strevens 1964:87ff.). So, in order to avoid misunderstandings I shall stick to MODALITY.

To sum up, the phrase "you bloody fool!" reflects three situational dimensions:

- GEOGRAPHICAL ORIGIN: it reveals that the speaker is British.
- SOCIAL ROLE RELATIONSHIP: it implies that the speaker considers himself as of equal social standing with the hearer.

- SOCIAL ATTITUDE: it shows that the speaker assumes that there is a relatively high degree of social proximity between himself and hearer.

Our proposed translation for this troublesome phrase will be revealed in due course. For the moment, however, some further exploration of the background considerations will be useful. It may be helpful now to link up our model of situational analysis with the psycholinguistic model of *top-down and bottom-up processes* referred to when analysing the process protocols in Chapter one. An utterance such as the one mentioned can be regarded as the bottom-up linguistic material, and the mental image of a situation such utterances evoke can be regarded as a top-down process. Thus in our case the phrase "bloody fool" uttered in this context provides the bottom-up material; and the experience which the speaker/hearer has of this phrase, as a result of having encountered it previously in a range of different situations, provides the top-down backcloth.

In Fillmore's terms, "bloody fool" is the *frame* which activates a *scene*, a situation, in this case, with all its relevant dimensions. The scenic quality of meaning becomes especially apparent in our example, because the whole Summerhill educational situation is evoked. As a *frame* "bloody fool" limits the types of situational dimensions to be recalled from our memory. A high degree of social distance, for instance, would not fit into the *frame,* and is indeed ruled out by the Summerhill scene. But what about the pejorative meaning of fool? It seems to be part of the frame, but is it really activated in the reader's mind? Is it part of the scene? I shall discuss this question in the passages to be considered next.

Having analysed the pupil's phrase and having briefly presented a model of situational and indeed psycholinguistic analysis, can we now translate it? What about the translation suggested by *DUDEN-OXFORD, Großwörterbuch Englisch:* "Du Vollidiot!" It raises doubts. Does this translation reflect any geographical origin? Does it really express that speaker and hearer have equal social roles, or does it show rather that the speaker feels to be "above" the hearer? Does it really suggest proximity, or is it not a rather hostile verdict creating distance? In a word, does it really activate the scene which was at the back of the author's mind? With the analytical model at our disposal so far we may well find it difficult to answer these questions, not only with reference to the German translation but also with reference to the original English utterance. It seems that our situational analysis is still lacking some important aspects. We have not considered the communicative function of the utterance, i. e. we have not asked what *speech act* is being performed, and we have not considered the *communicative function* of Neill's preface and the function of its translation.

3.2 Communicative functions of utterances, texts and translations

Ever since J.L.Austin delivered his famous lectures "How to do things with words" (Austin 1962), linguists have become more and more aware of the fact that saying something means performing actions. Austin coined the term *speech act* for this level of linguistic description. And for the speaker's intention when saying something the term *illocution* is now in common use, both for spoken and written language. Very often, however, we must infer a speaker's intention from the words he/she says. This is a problem for the linguist who has to develop rules to account for these inferencing processes, and this may also be a problem in everyday conversation, when utterances have a "non-literal" meaning and may thus create misunderstandings. For instance, if a wife, perhaps in the early stages of their married life, asks her husband during a car journey "Would you like a cup of coffee, dear?" her intention in our Western civilisation where women's language is ruled by a high degree of indirectness (cf. Tannen 1991:248ff.) is not really to ask him about his wishes and needs but rather to suggest that he should stop so that she can have some coffee. These meanings have to be learnt during the process of enculturation, as anthropologists call it, where one learns about the rules and norms governing our social behaviour.

These *social meanings* are determined to a large extent by the paralinguistic and non-linguistic conditions under which the utterances take place. Thus tone of voice, facial expression and gestures are important clues for getting at the social meaning behind the words. In written texts we normally do not have these clues and we must rely on our interpretation of the words within their contexts.

The fact that our process of comprehension is interpretive is the basic insight of psycholinguistic models, such as the notion of *top-down and bottom-up processes* and *scenes and frames*, mentioned above. Some theorists in translation studies have taken this idea as the point of departure for their theories. Thus Gutt (1990, passim) argues that translations are interpretive uses of language because the source text gives us no more than clues to what is meant, and in the comprehension process the historical, cultural and sociological background is needed to find out what these clues stand for or hint at. Gutt, in his basically hermeneutic approach, without explicitly stating the connection, takes up and adapts one of George Steiner's ideas, who says that translation is interpretation. This idea is stated the other way round by Steiner in his programmatic chapter on the translation of works of literature which he calls "Understanding as translation" (Steiner 1975:1ff.)

When dealing with individual utterances the speech act model can provide some insight into the comprehension process exactly along these lines, because when describing illocutions we interpret the speakers' intentions both from what they say and from the context in which the utterance takes place. Searle has described these interpretive processes in detail in his analysis of indirect speech acts (Searle 1975, passim).

What, then, is the pupil's intention, what does he mean to say or rather to do, when calling his teacher "a bloody fool?" In other words, what speech act does he perform? There is a large number of so-called *performative verbs* in every language serving as names for speech acts, according to Austin's estimate around 5,000 in English (Austin 1962: 150). Does the pupil want to abuse his teacher or does he want to contradict him or does he merely want to tease him putting himself at the same level with him? In the lines immediately preceding Neill's test there is some relevant information that might help to answer these questions:

> ..it is not only Neill that the kids treat with equality and fun and love; the whole staff are treated as pals and playmates. They do not stand on their dignity, nor do they expect any deference because they are adults. Socially, the only privilege the teachers have is their freedom from bedtime laws. Their food is that of the school community. They are addressed by their first names and seldom are given nicknames; and if they are, these are tokens of friendliness and equality. For thirty years, George Corkhill, our science master, was George or Corks or Corkie. Every pupil loved him.

First of all, the results of our situational analysis of the pupil's utterance are confirmed by this passage. "Equality" (line 1) is indeed mentioned as one of the principles of living together at Summerhill, and in the following lines this idea is further explained. There is, however, another feature which cannot so easily be deduced if we only look at the pupil's utterance on its own. There is a general attitude of friendliness and love between kids and teachers. Seen in this context the pupil's utterance is most likely not intended to *abuse* the teacher. It may be interpreted as *contradicting* or, more likely, simply *teasing*. Without going into the details of speech act theory we may also say that the pupil is performing one speech act by means of another (cf. Searle 1975, passim). He is teasing his teacher by contradicting him. The main thing is that his utterance is a sign of equality and also friendliness. It would be understood as such by a Summerhill teacher. It would certainly sound provocative when seen in a normal school situation, but not in Summerhill. When translating the phrase we must take care to consider these aspects. The translation "*Du Vollidiot!*" seems to be lacking that friendly, teasing note completely. I would suggest using a term frequently used by teenagers, which by the very frequency of its use has lost its provocative nature. What comes to mind is "*Blödmann!*" I concede, however, that this may be time-bound and become dated within a few years. Other words frequently used and not restricted to teenager slang are "*Schwachkopf*" and "*Dussel*".

Speech act theory has provided us with the tools for pinning down the function of the pupil's utterance. In terms of performative verbs, its function or illocution could be described as *teasing by contradicting*. In text analysis the *function* of a word, phrase, utterance or passage is the most important frame of reference. In text analysis there is a *hierarchy* of steps or aspects. Function is of the highest order. Once we have decided on the function all other considerations fall into place, as it were. Thus preserving the function here is certainly more important than preserving the TIME dimension.

In different contexts *bloody fool* would have a different function. Thus in a sentence like "Bill called John 'a bloody fool', whereupon John punched Bill on the nose" the illocution of *bloody fool* would be *abusing* and could indeed be translated by *Vollidiot.*

We have talked of functions of utterances, i.e. *illocutions.* For the description of these *illocutions* it is sometimes difficult to find single *performative verbs,* such as *ask, request, explain, abuse* etc. Thus for the description of the pupil's illocution I suggested the performative verb *tease,* but hastened to add that teasing here went hand in hand with an amiable attitude. In the same way, the sentence, "It is my test today, except that bloody - never a real swear word outside British realms - has been changed to a more popular expletive", could be described as a *statement* or, more specifically, an *addition* to what has been said before. But this description would still miss the main point of the utterance. Searle has warned that we must not expect there to be an individual performative verb for every speech act we encounter (Searle 1976: 2). There are cases where we have to resort to paraphrases. Nevertheless, we are somehow able to describe the speaker's communicative intention. Neill in his little follow-up does several things at the same time. He *adds* something to what he said, and he makes a *metacommunicative statement* about the possible international usage of an English word, and he *alludes to* a modern English four-letter word, which for taboo reasons he does not mention but leaves to the reader to imagine, thereby *adding a witty note* to his utterance. This is perhaps a rather exceptional case of performing several speech acts at the same time, but it seems that in real life conversations, utterances have more illocutions than speech act theorists have so far taken account of.

Obviously, a literal translation such as the one by Monika Kulow and Harry Rowohlt, does not render all the illocutions of the utterance, if it renders any illocution at all:

> Diesen Test mache ich heute noch, nur habe ich "blutig" - außerhalb britischer Gefilde ja kein echtes Schimpfwort - inzwischen durch ein populäres Füllsel ersetzt. (A.S. Neill, *Birnenstiel Neill,* tr. Monika Kulow and Harry Rowohlt, Reinbeck bei Hamburg, 1982)

Apart from the fact that "blutig", as we have seen, is not a swearword in German, this sentence does not make any sense at all. The translation of metacommunicative utterances poses problems because they refer to the linguistic material of the source language. It would only have made some sense if "bloody fool" had been inserted in brackets after the German translation in the preceding sentence and "bloody" had here remained untranslated. But even then the average German reader would not have been able to understand what Neill is referring to. He would not have been able to guess the four-letter word and thus would have missed the witty point of the utterance. And we all know that explaining witty sayings destroys their wit. For the German readership this utterance thus has no function, and therefore the best solution is to leave it out altogether.

Some people might argue that translators are not entitled to act in such an authoritarian way with an original text. Translators, it is often said, have to serve their authors, and must not change the text. One can only answer that they do not serve the author if they create a text which makes no sense to anybody. In other words, there are utterances which have a function only within the source language community. In such cases these utterances have no communicative purpose for the target language community. Furthermore, even if we leave out such a sentence we can still preserve the overall function of the text, in this case the preface of Neill's autobiography, the main purpose of which is to inform us about life at Summerhill (cf. our comments on a similar point in 1.3.4).

I mentioned above that it had been argued that translation is basically an interpretive use of language. In has become apparent in the last example that interpretation is further complicated by the fact that communication takes place between the writer of a source text and the reader of a target text, that is between members of two different cultures. In translation studies this fact is recognized in a number of models of the translation process, which I propose to call *functional models*. Hönig and Kussmaul (1982 passsim) have shown that cultural considerations help us to determine whether the function of the translation can be preserved or has to be altered. Reiss and Vermeer (1984) have suggested that the source text is merely a "Informationsangebot" (offer of information) from which the translator may choose, not at random, however, but with regard to the knowledge, needs and expectations of the target culture readers. It is the consideration of the target readers' needs, interests etc. which determines the purpose or function of the translation. In Reiss and Vermeer's terminology, a translation must be "*kohärent*" (coherent) with the situation of the target readers, and this situation determines the "*Skopos*", i.e. the goal or purpose, of the translation (cf. Reiss/Vermeer 1984:35ff.). Reiss and Vermeer use *coherence* in the same sense as Halliday and Hasan who distinguish between coherence and cohesion. A text is *coherent* with respect to the context of situation and it is *cohesive* with respect to itself. (Halliday/Hasan 1976:23). More recently, Gutt (1990) has proposed a similar model. Instead of coherence he uses the term *relevance*. The translator's decisions ought to be guided by considering what is relevant for the target reader. In Gutt's more detailed words:

> What the translator has to do in order to communicate successfully is to arrive at the intended interpretation of the original, and then determine in what respects his translation should interpretively resemble the original in order to be consistent with the principle of relevance for his target audience with its particular cognitive environment (Gutt 1990:157).

3.3 The cultural background

Neill's metalinguistic utterance shows that communicative acts are part of a *culture*, and this interrelatedness of texts with cultures have always caused problems for translators. Thus translators have had to decide if names of people or institutional terms not known in the target culture had to be explained or adapted, if allusions had to be made explicit or even dropped in the translation. There are no hard and fast rules for these decisions, although some may think there are (e.g. Newmark 1982:70ff.). As we have seen in the last example and as proposed by functional approaches to translation there is no other way for the translator but taking the trouble to start a chain of reflections, as it were, considering the function of the text-element within the overall text and the embeddedness of the text within its culture.

Cultural problems most often arise when there is a great distance between source and target cultures, such as between China and the western world. Thus the meaning of metaphors and symbols may create problems. For instance, in the west the dragon is usually a symbol of evil whereas in China it is a symbol of good luck. In the creation of symbolical and metaphorical meaning religion and mythology play important roles, and with distant cultures religions and mythologies are often very different. But even with apparently close cultures such as the British and the German culture we must be aware of potential differences even when such a popular text as the bible is concerned. P.G. Wodehouse in the *Code of the Woosters* describes the ill effects of too much drink by making a biblical allusion. He writes:

> I had been dreaming that some bounder was driving spikes through my head - not just ordinary spikes, as used by Jael the wife of Heber, but red-hot ones.
> (P.G. Wodehouse, *The Code of the Woosters*. Penguin 1967, first published 1938:p.5)

Now, as both in Germany and Britain Christianity forms an important part of the cultural heritage and since in both countries quotations from the Bible are common one might think that the reference to "Jael the wife of Heber" could be translated literally, but, in fact, it cannot. The story of Jael seems to be known to an educated British person with an average biblical knowledge, which may be seen from the fact that *Jael* is an entry in *Collins Concise Dictionary Plus* and explained as

> *Old Testament.* the women who killed Sisera when he took refuge in her tent (Judges 4:17-21).

In German encyclopaedias (e.g. *Der große Brockhaus, Meyers Enzyklopädisches Lexikon* or *Bertelsmann Universallexikon*), however, Jael is not mentioned, nor Heber either, which can be interpreted as a sign that the story is not part of an educated person's knowledge. A literal translation would, obviously, be of no use here, and an explanation would have to contain the whole story in order to evoke the *scene*, in Fillmore's sense, in the mind of the reader. This is a good example, by the way, that scenes are determined culturally. The *frame* ("Jael the wife of Heber") exists both in the British and German culture, but the scene is only evoked in readers of the British culture. What is the translator to do? The function of the allusion is first of all to intensify the metaphorical phrase "driving spikes through my head" used to describe the narrator's hangover. It may, in addition, have been used by Bertram, the main character and narrator, to "show off" his education. We would have to make a literary analysis of Bertram's character, though, in order to confirm this thesis. For the moment, let us take it for granted.

The first function, of intensifying, is, one might argue, to some extent also fulfilled by the addition "not just ordinary spikes...but red hot ones", and these words can easily be translated. If we want to preserve the second function, of "showing off", we will have to find a biblical or perhaps other story which is part of the average educated German person's cultural knowledge, because what the narrator alludes to here is not the Bible for the Bible's sake but the Bible as part of his culture's literary tradition. Unfortunately, there does not seem to be a biblical or indeed other story in German literature known to the average German reader which could be used to illustrate the notion of "spikes being driven through someone's head".

There are ways to solve cultural translation problems by the use of a functional approach, though. The narrator's allusion must be seen as part of his general way of speaking, and if after a more detailed analysis we find that allusions to the Bible or to other works of the cultural heritage are indeed typical of his speech we might then insert an allusion somewhere else in the story, a technique which has been suggested by Katharina Reiss and termed "*versetztes Äquivalent*" (equivalent transferred to another place, Reiss 1971:43). If we use this technique our translation will be in line with the overall tone of Bertram's way of narrating the story. We might also consider changing the image of spikes and using another simile to describe the pains of a hangover which could then be linked up with a different biblical or other well known story, for instance "Pains shot through his head like arrows through St. Sebastian's body". Thus here again, looking at the function of the phrase in question is hierarchically the most important aspect of analysis. Once we have decided on the function we may even change the semantics if the need arises.

There are, of course, cases where allusions or references to the source culture can or indeed must be replaced by target culture material. Replacement is the procedure advocated, for instance, by Nida for Bible translation. According to his principle of *dynamic equivalence* as opposed to *formal equivalence* (Nida 1964a:160) the translation of the Bible should read perfectly natural as if it was an original text. Culture-specific concepts of the source text will have to be substituted by target-culture concepts. The probably best known example is found in the Lord's Prayer where "Give us our daily bread" is translated into the Eskimo language as "Give us our daily fish." These are replacements caused by natural surroundings and ecology. The notion of "desert" produces problems in tropical countries and thus is often translated as "abandoned place". In some aboriginal New World cultures where "wheat" as a crop did not exist it was replaced by "maize" (cf. Nida 1964b:91ff.).

Nida did not use the concept of *scenes and frames*, which was developed much later. It could be applied here. One may say that although the *linguistic frames* are changed in the translation ("bread" becomes "fish", "desert" becomes "abandoned place", and "wheat" is changed into "maize"), the *mental scenes* nevertheless remain basically the same. Both "bread" and "fish" evoke the scene "basic type of food", both "desert" and "abandoned place" evoke the scene "solitary area", both "wheat" and "maize" evoke the scene "typical crop grown in a specific agriculture". Nida's concept of dynamic equivalence may be defined within the scenes and frames model as *difference of frames but similarity of scenes*.

Such differences in the material culture are perhaps more obvious than those in the social culture, when we have to know about people's attitudes, values, norms etc. An international firm which produced dishwashers wanted to sell its products in Argentina and had the advertising material, which had been very effective in the U.S.A, translated into Spanish. The tenor of the adverts was: "Get yourself a dishwasher and you'll have more leisure time for yourself!" The advertising campaign was a complete failure. In Argentina a housewife does not strive to have more spare time for herself, but her aim should be to have more time to spend on her husband and children. The adverts should have taken account of these social values (cf. Schmitt 1985:7).

To get back to the example quoted from Wodehouse, the specific allusion to the cultural background could not be substituted, because the literary cultures, although to some extent identical between Britain and Germany, did not overlap completely. There was no comparable biblical nor other story which would have been known by the average target reader. There are, of course, cases where we can preserve literary allusions with some modifications. A little earlier in Wodehouse's novel, at the beginning of the book, there is a dialogue between Bertram and his butler, which runs as follows:

> I reached out a hand from under the blankets, and rang the bell for Jeeves.
> "Good evening, Jeeves."
> "Good morning, sir."
> This surprised me.
> "Is it morning?"
> "Yes, sir."
> "Are you sure? It seems very dark outside."
> "There is a fog sir. If you will recollect, we are now in autumn - season of mists and mellow fruitfulness."
> "Season of what?"
> "Mists, sir, and mellow fruitfulness."
> "Oh? yes, I see. Well, be that as it may, get me one of those bracers of yours, will you?"
> (P.G. Wodehouse, *The Code of the Woosters*. Penguin 1967, first published 1938. p.5)

Shall we translate the butler's quotation of John Keats' *Ode to Autumn* rather literally as "*Zeit der Nebel und der reichen Fruchtbarkeit*"? Or shall we find a comparable line from a wellknown German poem such as "*graue Nebel wallen, kühler weht der Wind*" from Johann Gaudenz von Salis-Seewis *Herbstlied*, which every German schoolchild knows? Here again, considering the function of these lines within the text and within the translation will help us make our decisions. The topic of the novel is the typical way of life of the well-to-do British middle and upper classes, and the setting within the British culture is thus of great importance. The *Skopos*, to use Vermeer's term, is to translate the text as being firmly embedded within the British culture. Obviously, we cannot have Jeeves, the butler quote from a German poet like Salis-Seewis. This would not fit in with the British background. If we simply translated Keats into German, however, the German reader would not be able to recognize the quote because Keats' poem is not part of his cultural knowledge, and even if it was, he would only be able to recognize it if there was a standard German translation of it usually quoted, such as the translations of some of Shakespeare's famous lines. What preserves the function (British setting) in this case is inserting an explanation, not after the initial quotation, however, because then Bertrams subsequent question ("Season of what?") would be absurd, but after Jeeves has repeated the quote. Then an explanation would even fit in with Bertram's apparent illiteracy or poor memory caused by the hangover and the dialogue would here read:

"Was für eine Zeit?"
"Der Nebel und reichen Fruchtbarkeit - Keats!, sir"

What I am trying to show is that in each individual case we have to take text-function and target-culture into consideration. If we do not, our translation will not make sense, and we may even run the danger of being misunderstood.

Not so long ago a German politician's utterance caused some upheaval for precisely this reason. In 1986 the German chancellor Helmut Kohl was interviewed by *Newsweek* on how he judged the general secretary of the USSR Gorbachev and his intentions. Kohl's problematic utterances, quoted in most German newspapers, were:

Der war nie in Kalifornien, nie in Hollywood, aber er versteht was von Public Relations. Goebbels verstand auch was von Public Relations. Man muß doch die Dinge auf den Punkt bringen.
(Die Rheinpfalz, 7 November, 1986)

Now, comparing anyone with Goebbels is certainly not very tactful let alone diplomatic. Kohl should have known that. Such utterances are bound to be taken as an offence. Supposing in Kohl's favour that he was just thoughtless - and some people think that this is not untypical of him - the utterance and its illocution can be interpreted as an unintentional indirect speech act. Kohl *compared* Gorbachev with Goebbels and by this comparison *offended* Gorbachev.

This was bad enough, what made things worse was that in the English translation of Kohl's utterance an explanation was inserted:

Goebbels, one of those responsible for the crimes of the Hitler era, was an expert in public relations, too.
(Newsweek 27, October, 1986)

Kohl's interview had the effect that the Russians immediately cancelled their invitation for research minister Riesenhuber to come to Moscow. In the ensuing public discussion Kohl tried to explain that he never wanted to offend Gorbachev, that he did not even mean to compare him with Goebbels, and that the explanation after Goebbels' name had been inserted by Newsweek. Newsweek, however, maintained that the explanation had been inserted by German government spokesman Ost, who had thought that the explanation was necessary to make clear who Goebbels was. Ost, again, contradicted this and said he had suggested that the whole passage should be cut.

It was never really discovered who had inserted the disastrous explanation, but this is not the main point. The event is of methodological interest. Suppose spokesman Ost had really inserted the explanatory phrase, then he would not have taken into consideration that texts are embedded in cultures and that their effect (or function) is culturally determined. He had possibly internalized the rule, which is, in fact, prescribed by some teachers of translation, that names not known in the target culture must be explained. Obviously, such rules can have disastrous effect. Apart from grammar and some very closely defined cases of conventionality, one should be very careful about talking of rules in translation. Rules should be replaced by *strategies* which are based on considerations of the function of utterances within situations and cultures. Which are the strategies translators should use in cases such as these where culture plays an important part?

Let us use our example to answer this question in some detail. First of all, translators must interpret the function of the utterance in question, and they must then decide if they can or want to preserve it. If they do not want to, they must decide which of a number of new functions they want to fulfil. In our example this is rather tricky. We said above that the utterance was an unintentional offence. Shall we translate it as such? But Kohl, after having realized the disastrous effects of his remark, seems to have wished he had never made it. Thus in Kohl's interest the best decision would have been to cancel the utterance in the translation.

This decision is closely linked with what is usually the next strategic step, with cultural considerations. Translators have to be aware of the fact that readers' expectations, their norms and values, are influenced by culture and that their comprehension of utterances is to a large extent determined by these expectations, norms and values. In other words, these factors determine the *top-down processes*, and they take part in constituting the *scenes* which are created in the minds of the readers when they read a text. Explaining the names of Nazi politicians may be functionally adequate if, for instance, they appear in a history-book, because in these rather factual and impersonal texts we expect to get detailed information, which means that the text type influences our top-down processes and the scenes in our minds. Comparing someone in public with Nazi politicians, however, and even making the comparison more explicit, is, even 40 years after World War II, like breaking a taboo and will most certainly be offensive. Such utterances will immediately evoke a scene where the person compared is evaluated in an extremely negative way. So, if it was true what spokesman Ost said, namely that he had suggested that the whole passage should be cut, he would have done the right thing. The intended basic function of a positive characterisation of Gorbachev would have been preserved.

If we want to perform all the strategic analytical steps, we should also take into account the situation in which the original utterance took place. The situation was, above all, marked by MEDIUM. It was an interview and thus spoken language. Now, it is a well-known fact that in spoken language paralinguistic features such as tone of voice, facial expressions, gestures etc. add to the meaning of words. We do not have the video recording of the Newsweek interview, but it might very well be that an analysis of the videotape would have given us some further clue as to the meaning of Kohl's utterance.

It is one of the basic ideas of the functionalist approach and also of *Skopos*-theory (see below) that the function of the source text, and of course also of parts of the source text, can or must be changed, depending on the wishes, expectations, needs etc. of the target readers. Suppose that spokesman Ost had not inserted the explanation, but Newsweek had done so, then the English text is a good example of how translations can manipulate and change the function of the source text. A comparison which may originally have been intended to highlight a positive feature of the person referred to would then have been transformed into an aggressive and offensive act. Newsweek may have had its reasons for doing this, but we do not know them, and it would be futile to speculate about them.

By inserting bits here and there in the process of translation or also by leaving out information, the original function of the source text can be modified or completely changed. There are well known examples of this in literary translations. Some translations of Jonathan Swift's *Gulliver's Travels,* by leaving out allusions to 18th century England which target readers would not have been able to understand, changed the function from political satire to children's tale (cf. Reiss 1971:103f.). Similar things happened to some of Dickens' works. *A Christmas Carol, the Cricket on the Hearth, Sketches by Boz, Pictures from Italy, A Child's History of England* and *Pickwick Papers* were in an early stage of their reception in Germany translated for young people and for use in schools (cf. Drescher 1987:313). Bertolt Brecht transformed Shakespeare's *Coriolanus* into a play about the Marxist class-struggle by leaving out lines and passages of Tieck's translation and by purposely adding a few words in certain places (cf. Kussmaul 1974:76ff.). All these are examples of a special type of Skopos-oriented translation according to Reiss and Vermeer (1984), where the target culture, or at least the translator's ideas about the target culture, lead to a new function of a translation. Culture is thus the most comprehensive aspect when we make our decisions as translators, and one is indeed justified in saying that translation is intercultural communication (cf. Ammann 1989:39ff.).

Skopos theory has created some stir in translation studies, at least in Germany. It has sometimes been misunderstood. People maintained that the essence of the theory was changing the function of the original. Furthermore it was claimed that with such a theory at his disposal a translator could do with a text what he liked. This kind of criticism overlooks the fact that translators favouring Skopos theory, when deciding if they should preserve or change the function of the source text, do not act at random but consider the expectations and needs of their target culture readers. Moreover, although it provides the frames of reference for adaptations and modifications, the theory is by no means restricted to alterations and adaptations. It is of use even when we want to preserve the function and purpose of the source text. After all, the Skopos of our translation can be the faithful reproduction of the source text.

As we have seen, there are various possibilities for dealing with cultural implications. We can drop cultural allusions or references, we can replace them by target culture material and we can also make implied information more explicit. Unfortunately, at a practical level there are no hard and fast rules available for the translator to guide him or her as to which of these three strategies should be adopted in individual cases. The key thing is therefore that when confronted with a problem case, we should decide what the appropriate strategy should be and that the decision arrived at should be governed by the more far-reaching considerations of text-function within situation within culture.

3.4 Pragmatics and text types

I have tried to outline the various pragmatic frames of reference (situation, communicative function, culture) which can serve translators in making their decisions. There seem to be textual entities in languages where these frames of reference have produced conventional linguistic forms. I am referring to what is called *Textsorte* in German and which is normally, for want of a better word, translated into English as *text types*. As we have seen earlier MODALITY is closely related with text types, and names of text types bearing witness of this are: *business letter, instruction leaflet, student's textbook, scientific abstract, scholarly article, legal document, ordinance, regulation, weather report, job advert* etc. In professional translation, text types of the non-literary kind play an important part, and one would expect them to have been the object of translation studies. However, so far we have, it seems, been much more in favour of building "models" than studying text material on a contrastive basis (e.g. Reiss/Vermeer 1984, Chapter 11.). But some work has been done and some projects have been started (cf. Kvam 1985, 1992, Fabricius-Hansen 1991, Göpferich 1993), and there are studies by text-linguists and people concerned with Language for Special Purposes (LSP) which we can make use of and apply to translation (e.g. Baumann/Kalverkämper 1992, Clyne 1981, 1987, 1991, Gläser 1990, 1992, Schröder 1987a,b).

When studying text types within the framework I have outlined so far, special emphasis will have to be given to the question of how pragmatic dimensions such as culture and situation are reflected in text types. The influence of culture on text types has been recognized by a number of scholars (Clyne 1981, 1987, 1991, Galtung 1985, Gläser 1992, Schröder 1987a, 1987b), but to my knowledge the relation between situational dimensions and text types has not been systematically studied hitherto. I shall briefly try to sketch how such research, e.g. through students' M.A./ Ph.D./"Diplom"-theses, could be done.

In British scholarly articles and monographs, results are often introduced by the performative phrase *I suggest*. This can be interpreted as a sign of indirectness and reserve, a phenomenon which is described by Schröder (1987a) in scholarly texts under the concept of *hedging*. Hedging is used to soften and modify utterances, so that the speaker/writer does not run the risk of losing face when his position is undermined (Schröder 1987a:47).

In German scholarly texts we find greater directness. A typical phrase seems to be: "Wir können folgende Ergebnisse festhalten." These observations will, of course, have to be supported by corpus-based evidence. They seem to be in line, though, with Galtung's observations on intellectual discourse when he says that in the United States and in Britain critical statements are normally introduced by a few laudatory remarks. This could be interpreted as a type of hedging, in so far as the speaker "wraps up" his critical remarks and thus softens them in order to prevent a fellow academic losing face. German intellectuals, however, according to Galtung, immediately aim at the weakest point in the thesis being propounded and shoot the proponent down in flames (Galtung 1985:157f.).

In addition, when analyzing a corpus of scholarly texts on humanities subjects of 60,000 English words and 60,000 German words (cf. Kussmaul 1978a) I found that in the English texts there is less distance between writer and reader than in the German texts. The personal pronouns *I* and *we* in connection with certain speech acts seem to be quite common in English texts of this type whereas in German impersonal constructions abound. Thus the speech act *announce* in English texts usually has the form "I shall here deal with...". In German texts announcements typically have the form: "*Das vorliegende Kapitel/Buch will zeigen.../ Im vorliegenden Kapitel soll gezeigt werden...*" (The present chapter/book will show.../In the present chapter will be shown...) (cf. Kussmaul 1978a:55). Here again one could draw a parallel between these forms and a basic pattern of German intellectual discourse suggested by Galtung. He puts forward the hypothesis that German academic discussions do not take the form of dialogues but of parallel monologues and serve for self-affirmation rather than the joint search for new ideas (Galtung 1985:191).

We could try to apply the model of situational analysis referred to earlier in the chapter in order to describe the differences between the German and English text types. As far as SOCIAL ATTITUDE is concerned, in the English texts there is less distance, in the German texts there is greater distance. Hedging can be linked up with SOCIAL ROLE RELATIONSHIP. Hedging is a form of indirectness. If I suggest that something is the case but actually mean to state that it really is the case, I perform one speech act by means of another, which is the basic pattern of indirect speech acts (cf. Searle 1975, passim). Indirectness usually implies a lower-to-higher social role relationship. For instance, if we beg a favour of someone we act in a non-authoritarian way and use indirect requests such as "Could you pass me the salt?" We leave it to the hearer to accept the utterance as a request or as a question. In the same way, when suggesting that something is the case we leave it to the hearer to take the utterance either as a statement or merely as a suggestion. Thus in the English texts we find a lower-to-higher relationship whereas in the German texts we find a higher-to-lower or maybe equal-to-equal relationship. We ought to remember, though, that these are roles and not positions.

Calling to mind Fillmore's scenes and frames model once more it becomes apparent again that scenes differ from one culture to another. The situational or, more specifically, social "scene behind the texts", to quote Vannerem and Snell-Hornby (1986), is marked by different factors in the British and German culture.

The SOCIAL ATTITUDE features are possibly linked up with the PROVINCE dimension. It may very well be that "distance" in Germany and "closeness" in Britain is a typical feature of the academic communicative world. All this is, of course, hypothetical, and corpus-based studies would be of great help indeed in this area. Other forms of SOCIAL ROLE RELATIONSHIP may be relevant. The form of a lecture may vary when given for students and when given for colleagues at a conference. One would also have to take into consideration that other situational dimensions might be reflected in language. Thus TIME might be relevant in so far as linguistic conventions may change. Furthermore, SEX, a dimension not mentioned in the models quoted above, might also be reflected in language. Possibly male and female academics take up a different social attitude toward their colleagues, audience and readers. As far as indirectness is concerned, which seems to be linked up with hedging, it has been observed that it is a typically female form of behaviour (cf. Tannen 1991:187ff.,248ff.,283f.).

To sum up, contrastive studies should take both situation and culture into account. Potentially, all situational dimensions may determine the linguistic form of texts. When analysing text types it will be our task to find out which dimensions are the relevant ones. Culture must not be seen as a separate dimension but in relation to situational dimensions. In other words, in some situations there will be cultural influences, in others there will not. More specifically, we may expect that some situational dimensions such as SOCIAL ROLE

RELATIONSHIP and SOCIAL ATTITUDE are susceptible to cultural influences, because actions between people are governed by norms and conventions, and these in turn differ from one culture to another. For text types, this means that some text types, such as scholarly articles or scholarly discourse, are culture- specific, and others, e.g. instruction leaflets, as we shall see, are perhaps not. Contrastive studies of text types will be extremely useful for translation teaching, and we should encourage our students to work in this field in their (German) diploma, M.A. or Ph.D. theses. Once we know the specific conventions of text types we can use them as material for our syllabus. At the moment, however, we still have to rely on our intuition to a large extent.

3. 5 Instruction leaflets and manuals - a case study

As we have seen, text types such as scholarly papers and learned discussions, are, in all probability, systematically influenced by situational factors and culture, i.e. governed by conventions. This was observed even for close cultures such as Germany and Britain. When translating into distant cultures we must be even more aware of the fact that there may have to be modifications and changes of the original text. For example, when I discussed the translation of an instruction leaflet of a washing machine with Indonesian colleagues one of them suggested to me that the leaflet ought to be completely rewritten for the Indonesian market. A translation in the normal sense would not work really, because the readers of the leaflet in Germany and Indonesia belonged to two different social groups. In Germany and probably in the Western World in general, instruction leaflets are written for those who buy and use a washing machine. As the wages for manual labour are very high in these countries small jobs like installing the machine are done by the housewife's husband or even the housewife herself. Instructions for this reason have to be very detailed and explanatory. A layperson will sometimes want to know why instructions are given, because he/she does not know the technical details.

The situation in a developing country is different. Those who can afford to buy a washing machine do not perform manual jobs themselves. Since wages are low they have these jobs done by craftsmen or domestic servants. These people, however, have a completely different attitude toward texts, if they can read at all. Important for them are pictures. The actual written text may be shorter and less detailed. Some of the explanations may be unnecessary. For translations to work well in developing countries one will have to find out in the individual case who the readers of instruction manuals are and what one can expect of them.

After these "exotic" examples let us return to Europe and try to describe some of the conventions of English and German instruction leaflets and manuals.

I shall be concerned with one particular aspect. My hypothesis is that the various linguistic forms of the speech act *instruction,* or more precisely, its *illocutionary force indicating devices*, as Searle calls them (Searle 1969:62), or its *illocutionary force indicators*, to use a simpler term, are determined by text-typological conventions. Moreover, I would venture the hypothesis that there are co-occurrences between variants of illocutionary force indicators and specific contextual features within text types, so that, like in phonology, we might find combinatory variants or variants in complementary distribution. What I am, in fact, doing within speech act theory is trying to formulate a few *regulative rules* (cf. Searle 1969:33f.), i.e. rules which describe what is appropriate in a given situation, and which take the form "Do x" or "If y do x" (Searle 1969:34). Specifying Searle's general form for these rules "If y do x" they will have the logical form: "If there is a given text type y or a given context z within a text type y, then for directive speech acts use the illocutionary force indicator x."

For my investigation I used parallel texts (cf. Snell-Hornby 1988:86), in other words, I used original texts, and even if in some leaflets translations were to be found I did not use them because their illocutionary force indicators might have been influenced by the original texts. Altogether my corpus contained 20 leaflets and manuals of various length.

There is a need for these contrastive studies, because instructions can cause translation problems, as can be seen from the following example. In the English version of an instruction leaflet for bath salts we can read the following sentence:

> Balneum Hermal is added to the bath-water (not vice versa) and is well mixed

It would be interesting to observe the reaction of English readers. On the basis of its syntax the sentence can be interpreted as a statement that the well mixed baths salts are already part of the bath water. This is nonsense, of course, and the only thing the reader can do is try to understand the sentence in a way which makes sense in an instruction leaflet.

In the German original the sentence reads:

> Balneum Hermal wird in das Badewasser gegeben (nicht umgekehrt) und gut untergemischt

Although this sentence has the syntactic form of an affirmative clause normally used for statements it will be interpreted by the reader as an instruction. In German leaflets the passive voice, among other forms, is conventionally used as an illocutionary force indicator for instructions. In English leaflets, however, different forms are used. The most common one is the imperative. Thus an adequate translation would have been

Add Balneum Hermal to the bath water and stir well until dissolved. (This is the suggested translation of my colleague R.B.K.Sampson - patent pending!)

A translator must know these conventions, unless he/she wants to risk the break-down of communication. Those who teach translation often advise their students, when it comes to translating instruction leaflets, to use the imperative in English and the infinitive in German. In our example the variant would be

Balneum Hermal in das Badewasser geben (nicht umgekehrt) und gut vermischen

Following this advice may be a first step to avoiding a breakdown of communication, but it may lead to rather monotonous texts. If we look at instruction leaflets and manuals more closely, we will find that there are quite a large number of linguistic forms which serve to indicate instructions. In my corpus I found that in the English texts, apart from the imperative, there are

- please + imperative
- must + infinitive active
- must + infinitive passive
- have to
- it is advisable
- we recommend
- it is recommended
- it is important
- should

In the German texts, apart from the infinitive there are

- the imperative
- "bitte" + imperative
- "bitte" + infinitive
- present tense passive
- present tense active
- müssen
- "ist zu/sind zu"
- "wir empfehlen"
- "es ist empfehlenswert"
- "es ist ratsam"
- "sollte"

As a consequence of this variety, the relationship between text type and illocutionary force indicator is not as close as one might wish it to be. The German form "ist zu /sind zu" also appears in regulations, for instance, and German "müssen" and "sollte" can appear in a large number of everyday situations. This is also true for the English imperative. This means that there are a number of forms, whose presence or absence cannot be predicted in a given text type, and the term "convention" thus cannot be used in as strict a way as in other linguistic domains. There is, however, one form, which as an illocutionary device scarcely ever appears anywhere else but in instruction leaflets and manuals. This is the German infinitive. And there are also forms which never appear in instruction leaflets and manuals, such as indirect directives like "can you/could you/would you...etc. and hedged performatives like "I must ask you to". Although there is no one-to-one relationship between illocutionary force indicators and text types there are still tendencies. Within a given text type some forms are conventionally used, some are not, and a translator must have a knowledge of these forms.

The appearance and absence of certain forms can to some extent be explained by referring to *situation* and *scene*. Indirect directives are motivated by politeness and can thus be seen within the dimension of SOCIAL ROLE RELATIONSHIP. Forms of politeness are used when the relation, which may, of course, be role playing, is lower to higher. For this reason they are, for instance, used in business correspondence, and for the same reason they are absent in instruction leaflets and manuals. In these text types there is no need to adopt an inferior role when instructing someone, because the act to be performed, e.g. formatting a text, unlike paying an overdue bill, is not in the interest of the speaker/writer but in the interest of the hearer/reader. This type of role playing is thus not part of the make-up of the scene behind the text.

I suggested that there might be co-occurrences between illocutionary force indicators and specific contexts within text types. In the small corpus I used, I noticed that the German infinitive appeared when instructions were arranged in a sequence to indicate the individual steps of an action, e.g.

Entkalken Sie wie folgt:

- Wasserbehälter bis zur höchsten Anzeige mit Haushaltsessig füllen
- Kanne mit Deckel und Filterhalter mit Paperfilter einsetzen
- Wenn der Essig durchgelaufen ist, Kaffeemaschine ausschalten

In English sequences of this sort the imperative appeared, e.g.

Jacking instructions:
1. Remove the spare wheel, scissors jack and jackhandle from storage...
2. Pry off wheel cover by inserting the flat end of the jack handle across from the valve stem and twisting wrench
3. Loosen (but do not remove) the wheel nuts by turning them counterclockwise one turn while the wheel is still on the ground...

In the texts I examined, the German infinitive and the English imperative appeared in about nine out of ten cases in sequences of instructions. In German manuals of computer software, however, instead of the infinitives the imperative + "Sie" is used, e.g.

1. Suchen von Text:
2. Setzen Sie die Einfügemarke an den Punkt, an dem der Suchvorgang beginnen soll.
3. Wählen Sie den Befehl *Suchen* aus dem Menü *Suchen*
4. Geben Sie im Feld "Suchen nach:" den gewünschten Suchtext ein.
....

(Microsoft Windows. Handbuch 1985-1990)

It seems to me that this is a sign of ATTITUDE, i.e. a more intimate writer-reader relationship, and also of what House calls PARTICIPATION (House 1977, 44), i.e. inclusion of the partner, for instance by addressing him. In software manuals these forms seem to be conventional, but not in hardware manuals. In the German instruction manual of an Epson printer in sequences of instructions the infinitive can be found throughout. One cannot, of course, generalize from a few observations like these, but I think it would be worthwhile to examine a larger corpus and try to find out if ATTITUDE and PARTICIPATION manifest themselves linguistically, not only in the forms of speech acts but maybe also on other linguistic levels like syntax or lexis.

In English sequences of instructions there is no need to differentiate within the form of the illocutionary force indicator, because the imperative always includes the reader or hearer. But there may be other ways of creating a more personal ATTITUDE, like congratulations on the purchase of the product.

One might draw a tentative conclusion from these observations and suggest, in the form of Searle's regulative rules, that if the general tone of the instruction leaflet or manual is rather impersonal, then it is conventional to use infinitives in German sequences of instructions.

Both the German infinitive and the English imperative do not, however, occur in these contexts alone. Both are the most frequent illocutionary force indicators and appear in all sorts of contexts. Just as we cannot predict certain illocutionary devices for a given text type, we cannot predict certain illocutionary devices for specific contexts within text types.

As far as syntactic contexts are concerned, there is a tendency for certain structures to co-occur. After prepositional phrases in English texts we find "must" + infinitive, e.g.

For speeds in excess of 75 mph (120km/h) tires must be
inflated to the maximum pressure specified on the sidewall

The German equivalent in these contexts is the infinitive, e.g.

> Für Pflegeleichtprogramme nicht mehr als 1,5 kg eingeben

In German, active and passive declarative sentences seem to co-occur with instrumental prepositional phrases, e.g.

> Mit einem Strahl reinigen Sie die Zähne... Mit neun Strahlen massieren Sie jetzt das Zahnfleisch
> Mit dem Schiebeschalter... wird die Wasserzufuhr ein- und ausgeschaltet

The English equivalent is a gerund with instrumental function and a passive clause, e.g.

> The doors are locked by pushing in on the forward portion of the rocker lever

Here again we have no strict one-to-one correspondences between the linguistic form of the speech act and its immediate context. As we have seen in the previous examples the German passive affirmative clause can be used freely in instructive texts, and in the examples just quoted the imperative would always be possible. Nevertheless, we can, I think, talk about co-occurrence tendencies, because some combinations seem to be unacceptable, e.g.

> ? For speeds in excess of... tires are inflated
> ? Mit einem Strahl... müssen gereinigt werden
> ? Mit dem Schiebeschalter muß die Wasserzufuhr ein- und
>   ausgeschaltet werden
> ? The doors must be locked by pushing...

In translations these forms have to be avoided.

In the examples quoted so far the directive force of the illocutionary device was rather strong. Let us now look at phrases where this force is less strong, like in "we recommend"/"wir empfehlen" and the syntactic paraphrases "it is recommendable, it is recommended"/"es ist empfehlenswert, es empfiehlt sich, es wird empfohlen" and also phrases like "it is advisable"/ "es ist ratsam" and "should"/ "sollte". As these explicit illocutionary phrases suggest, the actions to be performed are not absolutely obligatory or necessary, and there is a marked co-ocurrence of these phrases with propositions specifying these non-obligatory types of actions. This is not surprising. What is interesting, however, is the co-occurrence of these phrases with immediately adjacent speech acts giving reasons, e.g.

> We also recommend the use of a cable release to eliminate even the last trace of camera vibration

> Es empfiehlt sich, einen Aufstellungsort zu wählen, an dem möglichst wenig Fremdlicht direkt von vorn auf den Bildschirm fallen kann, damit Farbverfälschungen und Lichtreflexe vermieden werden

The combination of *recommendations* with the *giving of reasons* can be explained if we think of the situations in which *instructions* or *recommendations* are normally uttered. *Instructions* just like *orders* usually imply a high degree of authority on the part of the speaker, in other words, the SOCIAL ROLE RELATIONSHIP between speaker and hearer is higher to lower. As a consequence there is no need to argue and give reasons why one wants something to be done. *Recommendations,* on the other hand, imply less authority on the part of the speaker, i.e. the relationship between speaker and hearer is equal to equal, or even lower to higher, and the giving of reasons, if one wants something to be done, seems appropriate.

In Searle's analysis of indirect speech acts there is an observation about the connection between recommendations and the giving of reasons. He says that one of the ways to utter indirect directives is by stating that there are good reasons for performing the action, e.g. "It would be a good idea if you left town" (Searle 1975:72) Without changing its illocution we can transform this sentence into the logical structure common in instruction leaflets: "I recommend you to leave town because it is a good idea". Searle's indirect statement-type recommendation can, in fact, also be found in our text-corpus:

Ihr Café Royal hält länger, wenn Sie ihn regelmäßig entkalken

Judging by the syntax this is a statement. It can be interpreted as a recommendation on the basis of Searle's type of indirectness. The increased durability of the machine is a good reason for the recommended action of decalcifying.

The conclusion to be drawn from these observations is a general communicative rule, which would also apply for translation: *When recommending give reasons for your recommendations.* It could be argued that this rule does not apply for instruction leaflets only but also for recommendations in other text types. In the light of the speaker-hearer relationship implied in recommendations and also in the light of Searle's observations this may very well be true, but further empirical studies of other text types will nevertheless be needed to substantiate this argument.

To someone who is looking for clear-cut distinctions my results may not seem very satisfactory. Some forms such as the German infinitive and the English imperative co-occur with many syntactic and pragmatic patterns, and for those forms which have a more restricted use there is still no regular co-occurrence with a specific context.

Furthermore, cultural patterns of behaviour do not seem to influence the form of instructions. Maybe instruction manuals and leaflets are not very susceptible to cultural influences because they deal with technical rather than social topics. We cannot expect that culture always influences our ways of communicating. The conventions described here are "purely linguistic". They are the forms idiomatically used to perform the speech act of instructing. Although we can logically apply Searle's regulative rule this does not mean that we are here faced with social behaviour similar to the one observable when, for instance, performing indirect directive speech acts. Cultural influences can be expected in situations where SOCIAL ROLE RELATIONSHIP and SOCIAL ATTITUDE are involved. The social roles people play are bound to be influenced by culture. Social role-playing, especially when adopting a lower-to-higher position, is closely influenced by rules of politeness and etiquette, as we have seen earlier in this chapter when discussing the *bloody fool* example, and the knowledge about how to be polite is part of a person's enculturation. In instruction leaflets, however, there is no need to be polite, because, as we saw earlier, the actions to be performed are in the reader's and user's own interest. Also, there is normally no need to adopt either an intimate or distant attitude, because factual information prevails, although there do seem to be special products such as computer software where in German manuals signs of intimacy can be observed.

I hope to have shown, however, that there are differences, although not cultural ones, between German and English instruction manuals and leaflets, and that it is important for translators to observe them. Until now these observations have been based on a small corpus of texts. Once it is enlarged, some of the few rules I found will have to be revised. I also hope to have shown some of the methodological problems we are confronted with when looking for conventions in text types, and as far as teaching is concerned, the aspects that have become apparent may sharpen our students' view when analysing text types.

3.6 Some didactic implications

In the think-aloud protocols (TAPs) reported on in the first Chapter, there was no evidence of how semi-professionals dealt with cultural implications of texts because the texts used were not culture-specific. TAP-experiments with such texts still have to be made. It could be seen on occasions, however, that the subjects had problems with other pragmatic dimensions, such as style, text type, the readership of the target text and the function of text-entities within a text. Some neglect of the stylistic and text type dimension, it will be remembered, became apparent in connection with fear of interferences, and a neglect of the function of text-entities and the role of the readership of the translation was evident in the misuse of world knowledge. Lörscher when analysing his protocols found that professional translators check their translations with regard to their stylistic and text type adequacy (Lörscher 1992b), and Jääskeläinen found that advanced students actually verbalize their reflections on the nature of the people who will be reading their translations (Jääskeläinen 1993:113). Considering the pragmatic dimension would thus be typically professional behaviour, and in our teaching we should therefore make use of pragmatic analysis in order to produce "functioning" translations.

I also mentioned in the first Chapter that error analysis can to some extent be used for finding out the reasons of errors. In the examples quoted in the present chapter it became evident that translators, even professional ones, had completely neglected pragmatic dimensions. Those who teach translation will have noticed that the consideration of these dimensions is a completely new idea for beginners, because many of them embark on translator training courses with the naive idea that translation means substituting the linguistic forms of the source language with linguistic forms of the target language. Pragmatic analysis will thus be indeed of remedial value.

We can sharpen our students' awareness of pragmatic dimensions, and this will help them produce a "functioning" translation. We have seen that for the proper functioning of a translation, text type conventions must be taken into account. It would be very helpful if these conventions and the differences between conventions in the source and target language were known. For this reason we should encourage corpus-based contrastive studies. Given the right guidelines such studies could be carried out, at least on a small scale, in seminar papers and, of course, also in Ph.D. theses. Research could be channelled so that our corpora would increase. Eventually we might be able to construct prototypes of text types, as suggested by Neubert (1984:68), and these prototypes could then be used for creating textbooks and other teaching material, and they might even be used in computer assisted translation in much the same way as terminology data banks.

I have tried to show that pragmatic considerations are of a hierarchical kind. The first and most important question to be asked is for the function of the linguistic unit we are dealing with in the source text. We then have to decide if we want to preserve, modify or change the function. But we cannot make these choices at random. Our decisions must depend on the expectations, needs, interests and knowledge of the target readers within a specific situation within a specific culture. Often these decisions will have been made for us by those who order the translation. For instance, a translator cannot just change the function of an instruction manual for a machine and produce a text that shows how instructions are written in the source culture but which does not enable the reader of the translation to use the machine. He can only do this if this was the special assignment given to him, perhaps in order to provide the material for producing a new target text. Normally, with instruction leaflets the function will be preserved, and the target readers will want to be able to use the equipment for which the instructions have been written.

Chapter 4

The analysis of meaning

4.0 Overview

Having discussed the most general frames of reference, i.e. pragmatic considerations, for our decisions as translators in the preceding chapter, let us now turn to more specific problems and look at the meaning of words. It will be seen that word meaning is not an isolated concept but closely related to the context in which the word occurs, to the user of the word and his/her intentions in a specific situation within a specific culture. This interrelatedness is at the centre of recent psycholinguistic approaches to the problem of meaning and comprehension. It will be discussed in section 4.1. It will be further illustrated by types of examples that have presented notorious translation problems (sections 4.2 - 4.4). This is followed by a concluding section on teaching implications which to adherents of a more traditional approach may perhaps sound somewhat revolutionary (section 4.5).

4.1 Meaning, comprehension and translation

In order to see more clearly how semantic problems in translation arise let us consider for a moment how the translation process works in straightforward cases. For instance, a simple sentence such as

(1a) She came into the room

will normally not cause difficulties, either in comprehending or in translating, and can be rendered in German without any effort by

(1b) Sie kam ins Zimmer.

In cases such as these, there is a close syntactic and semantic similarity between the sentence in the source language (SL) and the target language (TL), and these types of translations are generally regarded as "easy", because they can be produced without further reflection. But we must not underrate these quasi-automatic processes. They can be used to deal with much more complex translation tasks. They can, in fact, be used to deal with all those cases where we can resort to fixed syntactic patterns, idioms, stereotype metaphors, and textual conventions, and they are the result of training and experience and essential for speedy and economical professional work. They are internalized and routine processes (cf. Wilss 1989), and the skilled translator will be able to make use of them to a large extent.

It is when smooth understanding and reverbalization is blocked that translation problems arise. In accordance with psycholinguistic practice (cf. Hörmann 1981:102ff.) I shall, to begin with, distinguish between comprehension and production (=reproduction in translation) of linguistic utterances, although in translation, as we shall see, there is a close interaction between both activities. If we distinguish between them, however, we shall by the use of two separate categories be able to observe more phenomena.

Understanding and reproduction may be seemingly smooth and easy because the translator is not aware of problems which, in fact, do exist. As was pointed out earlier, self-awareness, which includes the ability to recognize problems, is one of the features of an experienced translator. If this ability is lacking, apparently smooth translation processes may result in blunders. Obvious cases, as we have seen, are interferences (cf. section 1.3.1).

There can be several reasons for interruptions in the comprehension process. Firstly, and perhaps most commonly, it may happen that when translating from the foreign language we come across a word which we do not know at all and the meaning of which is not clear from the context. Secondly, we may seem to know the word, but its meaning in the specific context is not known to us. Thirdly, a word may be used in a highly idiosyncratic way by the author, and finally, a word may seem not fit into the context at all. I shall deal with these questions in this and the next chapter.

Understanding may work smoothly, but there can still be problems with reverbalization. When translating into the foreign language, we may have difficulties because our lexical and semantic knowledge is not large enough. Both when translating into the foreign language and into the mother tongue a "literal" translation may not be possible, in other words, one-to-one correspondences between SL-words and TL-words like in example 1a) and 1b) will not be available, and we will have to resort to translation shifts and paraphrases.

In all of these cases the translator has to switch from automatic reflex to reflection, as Hönig calls it (Hönig 1986:230ff.), and text analysis comes into play. We have seen in the preceding chapter that the most important question concerning the analysis of a text to be clarified before we start translating is the function of the passage in question and the overall purpose of our translation, which is determined by the receptors of the translation in their specific situation within a specific culture. Once function and purpose have been determined, however, there still remains much thinking to be done, and this is where the problems often really start. Potentially, the original functional and purpose-governed decisions have consequences on all linguistic levels: the translation of words, the rendering of syntax and cohesion between sentences. Let us consider the consequences of functional decisions for the translation of words. Words and their meaning present, as any teacher of translation will have experienced, the most frequent problems to be solved.

As far as meaning is concerned there has been a strong influence of structural semantics on translation studies. Componential analysis has proved to be extremely valuable in providing a firm methodological basis for the solution of meaning problems. The works of Nida and Nida/Taber can be quoted here as now classic approaches (cf. Nida 1964, Chapters 3-5; Nida/Taber 1969, Chapters 4 and 5). There is an inherent danger in this approach, however. It may lead to an undue emphasis on the word as an individual unit. This seems to have been felt by Newmark who distinguishes between communicative and semantic translation in order to be able to take account both of the individual word and the text (Newmark 1981:18ff., 62ff.). From a functionalist point of view, however, this dichotomy is no longer necessary. Semantic translation always serves communicative goals, and communicative translation always considers the semantic potential of individual words. As we shall see, there can be a synthesis of these seemingly opposing categories, if we do not restrict ourselves to one model of linguistic analysis. Componential analysis should be complemented by psycholinguistic approaches and by linguistic pragmatics.

What, then, are translators supposed to do when they encounter problems with the translation of words? First of all, they should not regard a word as a dictionary entry only, which can be subdivided into a number of definitions or meanings which in turn can be analysed according to semantic features or components. Further, it should not be their aim to preserve the features of the meaning of a word at all costs. They should rather ask questions like: What are the relevant features of the meaning of a word in a given context with regard to the function of the translation? This sort of question is not as obvious as it might seem; at least it does not appear to be so for many translators. Naive language users and, I am afraid, many translators and also teachers of translation seem to be of the opinion that words per se have meaning. This may even be true for not so naive people who are preoccupied with componential analysis. They, for instance, typically ask questions like: "What is the meaning of 'bustle'"? The - provocative - answer should be: "It has no meaning. I cannot tell you unless you tell me more about the context in which the word is used." The person who asks such questions is thinking of words as isolated units, and such a viewpoint continues to be found even amongst experienced translators as we shall now see. Words as lexical units, it should be emphasized, have only a potential meaning, and its is through the context that this potential is realized.

In his short story *The Open Window,* Saki describes how a young man called Framton is paying his first visit to a certain Mrs. Sappleton (for the example see Hönig and Kussmaul 1982:102) While waiting for her to appear, he talks to her niece who tells him about a terrible accident that had recently happened to her aunt's family. Eventually, Mrs. Sappleton appears, and the young girl interrupts her tale:

> (2a) She broke off with a little shudder. It was a relief to Framton when the aunt bustled into the room with a whirl of apologies for being late in making her appearance.
> (Elisabeth Schnack, ed. *Englische Gruselgeschichten. Uncanny Stories.* München: dtv 1981:102+104)

The German translation by Elisabeth Schnack reads as follows:

> (2b) Mit einem kleinen Schauder brach sie ab. Framton empfand es wie eine Erleichterung, als die Tante endlich unter einem Schwall von Entschuldigungen, weil sie so spät erschiene, ins Zimmer gestürmt kam.
> (Elisabeth Schnack, ed. *Englische Gruselgeschichten. Uncanny Stories.* München: dtv 1981:103+105)

Let us look at the translation of "bustled" by "stürmen", which could be back-translated into English by "rush" and which may be seen as a modification of "came" in example (1a), and let us try to imagine how the translator might have proceeded in this case. Let us suppose that her smooth process of understanding was interrupted because she did not know the precise meaning of "bustle" and had to look up the word in a dictionary. Let us further suppose in her favour that she was not content with what she found in a bilingual dictionary, and that she consulted a monolingual one. She could have found some information such as

> "bustle (cause to) move quickly and excitedly: Tell him to bustle, hurry. Everyone was bustling about / in and out, appearing to be very busy" (ALD). "bustle to be busy, often with much noise: She is bustling about the house" (Dictionary of Contemporary English, DCE).

Now, for translators, and above all for students training to be translators, and even for some teachers of translation, there seems to exist an inviolable maxim which I have hinted at above and which goes: Try to preserve as many aspects (features, components) of the meaning of a word as you possibly can. Translators seem to follow this maxim especially when they have to look up a word in a dictionary, and for the definition found in a monolingual dictionary they then try to find an optimally precise equivalent in the target language. Since students, owing to their deficiencies in the foreign language, have to consult dictionaries very often they usually find the above-mentioned maxim very attractive. The translator of our short story seems to have followed this maxim too. In translating "bustle" by "stürmen" she actually preserved quite a number of semantic features, namely NOISY, SPEEDY, EXCITED, and in doing this she was in fact doing what a famous translation theorist suggested. When Nida talks about meaning and translation he says: "What we do aim at is a faithful reproduction of the bundles of componential features." (Nida 1974:50)

Let me deal with Nida's principle for a moment, because it seems still to be very much in favour with teachers of translation. Thus Larson takes up Nida's suggestion and talks about "words as bundles of meaning" (Larson 1984:55ff.). It is certainly a step in the right direction if we teach our students to "unpack" the meaning of words, because it helps them to overcome the naive notion that words and things are the same, and that there must always be equivalences on the word level between two languages. It is a step in the right direction but one should take some further steps. Larson asks her students to "restate" the meanings of individual words, "indicating all of the concepts which are included" (Larson 1984:62), and in her exercises she uses isolated words or at best isolated sentences. Comprehending the meaning of a word, however, as psycholinguistic research has shown, is a dynamic process. Meaning is created by the potential concepts of a word and at the same time by the context or situation in which the word is used and which determines to what extent the potential concepts are being activated in the reader's mind. Let us try to retrace the comprehension and, indeed, translation process in the case of "bustle".

Our translator has reproduced quite a large bundle of componential features of "bustle", but she has not reproduced the important one. In order to be able to do this she should have stopped focussing her attention solely on the individual word and should have taken a look at the context. She should have asked herself: What is the function of this passage and which are the relevant features of "bustle" with respect to this function? In other words: How do we comprehend this sentence?

The actions of Mrs. Sappleton have to fit in with her general character and nature. There must be no inconsistencies. Mrs. Sappleton, as we learn from the story, is a middle-aged lady to whom conventions and etiquette seem very important. She has kept her visitor waiting, either because she was busy or, more likely, because she thought it was more becoming not to show undue haste. One could never use "stürmen" of a person like her, in no context whatever. When Mrs. Sappleton is described as "bustling into the room" the reader does not really associate the features NOISY, SPEEDY, EXCITED in his mind at all, but merely the feature BUSY. This feature, however, is not part of the make-up of the German word "stürmen". What is worse, "stürmen" possesses additional features which do not fit in with the lady's behaviour at all. It implies forcefulness and very high speed and is thus not a suitable translation of "bustle" in this context. A translation which takes into account context and function might read:

(2c) ...als die Tante endlich ... geschäftig das Zimmer betrat /ins Zimmer kam.

We have not reproduced a bundle of componential features, in Nida's and Larson's terms. We have only reproduced one single feature of the meaning of the SL-word. For the purpose of our text, however, this is exactly what is needed. Our translation is sufficiently precise.

There is no single word in German which combines the features WALKING and BUSILY, and we thus have to use a paraphrase for our translation. We have seen earlier, in the analyses of our TAPs, that paraphrases were sometimes not regarded by the students as real translations (cf. section 1.3.6). Paraphrasing, evidently, is the most common translation technique when there are no formal equivalents, and we should encourage our students to make use of it, maybe even in cases where there actually are formal equivalents, in order to root the idea in their minds that paraphrases are indeed proper translations.

I mentioned above that there is a close interaction between comprehension and production of linguistic utterances. Our comprehension of "bustle" within the context of the story is, in fact, verbalized via a paraphrase, and the paraphrase turns out to be the best translation.

What we have been doing here is combining the psycholinguistic model of *top-down* and *bottom-up* processing described earlier with the structuralist model of semantic feature analysis, and this combination is exactly in line with the functional approach to text analysis in translation studies. One may say that the function of a word is indeed the activation of its meaning potential by the context in which it is used.

The context of the story provides the necessary background, the *top-down knowledge*, for the understanding of the *bottom-up material*, i.e. the word "bustle" with all its semantic features. Psycholinguistic research has shown that, in the process of understanding, only those semantic features of words are *activated*, to use Fillmore's (1977a) and also Hörmann's (1981) term, which are relevant in a given context. There is a very illustrative example provided by Barcley et al.(1974) and quoted by Hörmann (1981:139). The word "piano" has, potentially, quite a number of semantic features: HEAVY, WOODEN, SOUND-PRODUCING, BEAUTIFUL etc. If, however, a person hears or reads the sentences

1. The man lifted the piano
2. The man smashed the piano
3. The man tuned the piano
4. The man photographed the piano

the verbs in turn activate one of the various features which make up the meaning of "piano". The first sentence activates the feature HEAVY, the second activates WOODEN, the third SOUND-PRODUCING and the fourth BEAUTIFUL (Barcley et al. 1974:476, Hörmann 1981:139). In other words: bottom-up processes which are set into motion by the potential semantic features of "piano" are counterbalanced by top-down processes which are started by the different verbs.

A more comprehensive way of explaining the process of understanding is offered by Fillmore's (1976, 1977a, 1977b) *scenes-and-frames model* mentioned earlier in connection with situational analysis. We can here use his model for explaining the comprehension of word meaning, a purpose for which his model was, in fact, originally used.

If we apply Fillmore's model to our understanding of "bustle" in the example quoted, we may say that in the preceding part of the story a scene has been activated where, in an elegant house a visitor is waiting for the lady of the house to appear while he is being entertained by a young girl. The entrance of the lady is part of that "scene", and the way she comes into the room must fit in with the general situation that has been evoked in the reader by the words of the narrator. Perhaps there are cultures where such actions as "stürmen" are typical in these situations. Within the British culture where, at least in the days when the story was written, the ideal of genteelness still flourished it would be hard to imagine this happening.

In my teaching I find the metaphorical notion of *scene* very useful in explaining the comprehension process when cultural experience (e.g. the genteelness ideal) is involved. I also find its metaphorical quality useful for understanding the meaning of abstract words. Making students aware of concrete experiences, which can be regarded as part of a scene, may help them understand abstract concepts and find suitable translations. For instance, in a text on the causes and cures of back-pain, students had to translate the passage:

> (3a) Man is a vertebrate, which means he has a backbone, or spine. The spine has
> a number of important functions in man's existence, not the least of which is the
> role it plays as the basis and core of the back.
> (Leon Root and Thomas Kiernan, *Oh, My Aching Back,* New York 1975: p.3)

A translation suggested initially by the students for the last two lines was

> (3b) ...eine der wichtigsten Funktionen ist seine (des Rückgrats) Rolle als
> Grundlage und Kern des Rückens.

In this rather literal translation the words "basis" and "core" were regarded as isolated units and equivalents were used which may fit in other contexts but not in this one. "Grundlage" suggests horizontality whereas the human spine is vertical, and "Kern" suggests interiority whereas the spine is central. In order to stimulate a better translation I tried to make the students aware of what as human beings they knew of their backs, of the way it was built anatomically, with the spine running down from the head to the pelvis, and of what would happen if it suddenly collapsed. In other words, I tried to describe a scene in Fillmore's sense. As a result, the students came up with the much more appropriate translation:

> (3c) ...eine der wichtigsten Funktionen ist seine Rolle als Stütze und Hauptbestandteil des Rückens

It will depend on the teaching situation which model we apply to rationalize our comprehension processes, be it the rather general notion of top-down and bottom-up processes or the activation-of-semantic-features model or the scenes-and-frames model. All of them make it quite clear that comprehension is a dynamic process, an interplay between our knowledge, our experience and our expectations on the one hand and the linguistic utterances we hear or read on the other.

The maxim mentioned above, which seems to have been adopted by many translators and teachers of translation and which says that there should be a complete reproduction of all the componential features of a word, can now be replaced by a new maxim which corresponds to the process of understanding utterances in texts in a much better way and which is much more in line with what should happen in translating. This maxim could be defined as: try to reproduce just that semantic feature or just those features which is/are relevant in a given context with regard to the function of your translation. This maxim we have called the "*maxim of the sufficient degree of precision*" (cf. Hönig and Kussmaul 1982:58ff.).

This maxim seems to be in line with some of Grice's by now rather famous *conversational maxims* (Grice 1975), namely the *maxim of quantity* and the closely related *maxim of relevance*, which are made use of as a theoretical basis by Hatim and Mason when discussing effectiveness and efficiency in translation (Hatim/Mason 1990:94, cf. also Baker 1992:225ff.). The maxim of quantity runs:

> Make your contribution as informative as required (for the current purposes of the exchange). Do not make your contribution more informative than is required. (Grice 1975:45)

And the maxim of relevance is simply stated as:

> Be relevant. (Grice 1975:469)

Suppose we had translated "bustle" in our example by "als die Tante mit raschen Schritten ziemlich geräuschvoll, energisch und geschäftig das Zimmer betrat", then the reader would perhaps have been lead to think that the manner in which the aunt entered the room was an important point in the story, an expectation which, of course, is not fulfilled.

It could be argued, and in fact some of my colleagues in discussion have done so, that we do not need "outdated" semantic feature analysis at all to understand the meanings of words in texts. It is much quicker and more economical, so they say, to look at the relevant context, and thus, for instance in accordance with Fillmore's scenes-frames model and Grice's principles, settle on the relevant meaning of a given word. There seems to be a tendency observable especially in the functionalists in translation studies (Vermeer, Ammann, Holz-Mänttäri, Hönig, to name but a few) to prefer this purely contextual approach.

I think one should be careful not to throw out the baby with the bath water. It would be short-sighted to maintain that we can always guess the meaning of words from the context in which they are used. If this was the case, surely no new information could be given. We should also bear in mind that, when translating, we often come across or look for words the meaning of which we do not know or only partly know. Suppose we did not know the meaning of "bustle" and we tried to guess its meaning from the context, it would be very unlikely that we would be able to translate it by something more specific than *kommen* (come). In cases such as these structuralist semantic models of meaning-analysis can still be very useful.

Besides, these structuralist models are still the main basis for the making of dictionaries, and since dictionaries are the main tools of translators, it is perhaps not a bad idea to have a knowledge of the semantic principles according to which dictionary entries are structured. A word for a translator is, alas, often a form which has no meaning unless he looks it up in a dictionary. Words, when translating, are often frames which do not activate scenes, because the frames are strange and unfamiliar. I shall talk about the use of dictionaries in the next chapter.

Seen from a structuralist point of view, then, the problems involved in the translation of a word like "bustle" represent the most common type of semantic problem. The meaning of comparable words in different languages only correspond exactly in very rare cases. This is because different language systems structure reality in distinct ways. In more precise terms, the semantic features of the meanings of words of two languages usually do not correspond completely. There are always one or more features which are not part of the supposedly corresponding meaning of a word in the other language. We are here faced with a well-known phenomenon in structuralist semantics, *partial overlapping of meaning*.

What is important from a psycholinguistic point of view, however, is the discovery that meaning is not something static and that, in translating, the size of the overlapping area has to be determined in each individual case. The process of understanding and translating, as demonstrated by the example of "bustle", might be described as *foregrounding of semantic features* of words, which, as we have already observed, means that at the same time some semantic features have to remain in the background.

4.2 "Bedroom" - a prototypical case

We have so far concentrated on the process of activation of semantic features in understanding. Let us now turn in more detail to the complementary process, the *suppression of semantic features*. In Oscar Wilde's *The Importance of being Earnest* there is a scene where Lady Bracknell has just received the surprising news that Jack wants to marry her niece Gwendolen. Lady Bracknell immediately starts to interrogate him about his character and his financial situation, and in the course of this Jack mentions that he possesses a country house. Lady Bracknell's interest is instantly aroused and she exclaims:

> (4a) A country house! How many bedrooms?
> (Oscar Wilde. *Play*. Harmondsworth: Penguin 1954:267)

In a recent translation by Peter Zadek and Gottfried Greifenhagen this is rendered in the same way as it was translated earlier by Franz Blei, namely as:

> (4b) Ein Landhaus! Wieviele Schlafzimmer?
> (Oscar Wilde. *Bunbury. Erstdruck der Übersetzung von Peter Zadek und Gottfried Greifenhagen in: 2. Programmheft Freie Volksbühne Berlin, Heft 4,1979/80:23)*

Now, why does Lady Bracknell in Oscar Wilde's play want to know about the number of bedrooms? Because the number of bedrooms is a conventional measure of the size of a house. The fact that the rooms are referred to as having a bed in them is of no importance really. Lady Bracknell wants to know how big the house is, and this is a very important question, since the bigger the house the more welcome Jack will be as a potential husband for her niece.

The German translation sounds rather strange in this respect. Referring to the size of a house by mentioning the number of bedrooms is not the normal thing to do in Germany. The word "Schlafzimmer" always means that the room is used exclusively for sleeping in. Children's bedrooms, for instance, are not called "Kinderschlafzimmer" but "Kinderzimmer", and the word implies that these rooms are also used for purposes other than sleeping in. Thus the readers or the audience of the German version of Wilde's play might ask themselves: Why is the old lady so interested in rooms with beds? Does she mean to hint at the amorous activities of a bachelor? The German translation has thus a totally different meaning from the original (cf. also Baker 1992:239 on similar effects in Switzerland).

The faulty translation can easily be explained. The translators contented themselves with having found a formally equivalent compound. They translated the English compound by a German compound, naively believing that their translation was precise enough since every part of the SL-word was represented in the TL-word. The semantics of *bedroom* are not that simple, though. In the English compound *bedroom* the semantic feature CONTAINING A BED is made explicit, and this feature is activated in some contexts but not in all. In a context like "after supper the couple retired to their bedroom" the feature CON-TAINING A BED is doubtlessly activated by the reader or listener, but in the context of Oscar Wilde's play this feature is not activated by the reader or thea-tre audience at all. One might say that the feature CONTAINING A BED is *neutralized or suppressed* in a context such as this.

There is another typical situation, mentioned by Kupsch-Losereit (1986: 14), where such suppression takes place but where it often is not realized in translations. American army officers in Germany were looking for apartments by putting up notices in a south German newspaper which ran: "Amerik. Off. sucht 4 Schlafzimmer in KL-West" or "Amerik. Off. sucht App. (3 Schlafzimmer)". Here again the person looking for an apartment was not aware of the fact, that in Germany the size of apartments and houses is not referred to by the number of bedrooms, but by the number of rooms in general. A proper advertisement should have read: "Amerik. Off. sucht 5-Zimmer-Wohnung" or "...sucht 3-Zimmer-Wohnung".

The tendency to translate "bedroom" by its German formally equivalent compound "Schlafzimmer" can be explained by Fillmore's scenes-frames model. The translators, all of them non-native speakers of English, activated a scene which was prototypical in their German cultural experience, namely a scenario where a bed, sleeping and night is part of the make-up. One might even argue that this is indeed the prototypical English scene for "bedroom". This is also the scene which, perhaps with a few more details which I will leave to the reader's imagination, is activated by the sentence just quoted: "After sup-per the couple retired to their bedroom". The not so prototypical scene behind the frame of Lady Bracknell's utterance was apparently not part of the experi-ence of the non-native speakers of English, and they therefore failed to interpret it correctly from the text.

I have used "prototypical" when referring to the scene evoked by "bedroom". The notion of *prototypes* in semantics is closely associated with the work of Eleanor Rosch (1973) and, more recently, with that of George Lakoff (1987), and has been discussed within the field of translation studies, for in-stance by Mary Snell-Hornby (1988) and Brigitte Handwerker (1988). It is based on the idea that when comprehending and producing utterances we do not have a checklist of semantic features in our minds, but we think in holistic notions which are determined by our experiences. As a result, linguistic categories have a *hard core* and *blurred or fuzzy edges*. Rosch's examples have become classical. In Rosch's experiments subjects judged certain members of a category as being more representative than other members. For instance, robins are judged to be more representative of the category "bird" than are chickens, penguins, and ostriches. The most representative members are called "prototypical" members. An ostrich is not a prototypical member but belongs to the fuzzy edge of the category (Rosch quoted from Lakoff 1987:41).

The thing to notice about these categories is that they are determined by culture. For instance, for some African tribes ostriches may be typical birds because they are part of their daily experience. In the same way the notions associated with "bedroom" and "Schlafzimmer" respectively may vary between the German culture and the Anglo-Saxon cultures. There seems to be a hard core, such as a bed or bed-settee as far as furniture is concerned, but at the fuzzy edges there seems to be a greater variety of additional furniture in British and American bedrooms. Moreover, the purposes of the room seem to differ. The room appears to be used in Germany predominantly for sleeping, but in Britain and the US also for other activities such as studying, listening to music etc. In translation we will have to decide which aspects of the notion of this word must be translated, the core or the core plus fuzzy edges or the fuzzy edges alone. The notion *of suppression and foregrounding of semantic features* which we have used above is very much in line with a prototype approach to word meaning. One might say that the prototype approach makes us aware of the fact that word meaning has to do with experience. Features of the meanings of words depend on our cultural experiences and, as the scenes-and-frames model suggests, also on our experience as determined by situation and context. Culture, situation and context will thus determine which of the components of the meaning of a particular word will be preserved and which will not.

There is a hint at the core-and-fuzzy-edges structure of *bedroom* in the definition given in *Webster's Third New International Dictionary:* "a room furnished with a bed and intended primarily to be slept in", and also in *Collins COBUILD English Language Dictionary* "a room which is used mainly for sleeping in". "Primarily" and "mainly" could be understood in such a way that *bedroom* is a room that can be used for other purposes as well as sleeping in, and the definition thereby seems to hint at the fuzzy edges of the concept. The fuzzy edge of *bedroom* would, depending on context, be translated into German as "Kinderzimmer", "Gästezimmer", "Jugendzimmer", or simply as "Zimmer".

Rainer Kohlmayer in his relatively recent translation of Wilde's play seems to have taken account of the fuzzy-edges-structure of the word. He writes:

(4c) Ein Landhaus! Wieviele Zimmer?
(Oscar Wilde. *Bunbury*. Stuttgart: Reclam 1981:23)

Here the translator has not been deceived by the form of the word but has reproduced its meaning in the given context in a sufficiently pertinent way, thereby evoking the in the reader or audience the "scene" which Lady Bracknell actually had in mind.

My analysis of the meaning of bedroom is corroborated by a passage from John Braine, *Room at the Top,* which was brought to my attention by Petra Schwenderling. The narrator in this passage makes fun of his uncle's and aunt's concept of "bedroom" which was exactly in line with a literal understanding of the word where the meaning is understood from the two parts of the compound.

> My room at Eagle Road was the first room of my own in the real sense of the word. I don't count my cubicle in the N.C.O.'s quarters at Frinton Bassett because I hardly ever used it except for sleeping; and I always had the feeling that it had been made impersonal by the very number of others there before me, living on the verge of departure to another station or death. Nor do I count my room at my Aunt Emily's; it was strictly a bedroom. I suppose that I might have bought some furniture and had an electric fan installed, but neither my uncle nor my aunt would have understood the desire for privacy. To them a bedroom was a room with a bed - a brass-railed one with a flock mattress in my case - and a wardrobe and a hard-backed chair, and its one purpose was sleep. You read and wrote and talked and listened to the wireless in the living-room. It was as if the names of rooms were taken quite literally.
> (John Braine. *Room at the Top.* Penguin Books 1959:11)

4.3 Similar Cases

The phenomenon of *suppression of semantic features*, which I have illustrated and which becomes apparent through translation together with the *foregrounding of semantic features*, are frequent processes in comprehension and translation. They are highlighted in forms such as "bedroom". In order to show how we decide which features are to be suppressed or foregrounded I shall discuss a number of similar forms.

When translating the word *Roman Catholic* into German, for instance, *katholisch* will do on most occasions. *Multi-storey car park* will usually be translated by *Parkhaus*. *Greenfly* and *blackfly* will usually both be translated by *Blattlaus*.

There may be situations, however, when we will have to be more precise, and this is where the function of the words within their surrounding context and also the function of our translation plays an important part. If in the case of our first example our text is not a general description of a person but an official document we will have to translate *Roman Catholic* by *römisch-katholisch*. If

multi-storey car park appears in a report of various types of car parks we may
have to translate it as *Parkhochhaus,* and if *greenfly* and *blackfly* appear in an
instructive text written for gardeners about the possibilities of using various
insecticides we will have to be more precise and translate *grüne Blattlaus* and
schwarze Blattlaus respectively.

In the examples just quoted, the TL-word, depending on the function of
our translation, specified less semantic features than the SL-word. Of course
there is also the reverse case, which may be illustrated by the English word
partner in a newspaper article:

> (5)Then there are the more serious strains. If a parent, a partner or a close
> friend dies, the bereavement takes its toll of our mental and physical
> health.
> *(The Sunday Times Magazine, May 28, 1978)*

If one had to translate this text into German the formal equivalent *Partner* would
not be sufficiently precise. The context suggests that the meaning of engl.
partner here contains features such as MEMBER OF THE OPPOSITE SEX,
PRIVATE RELATIONSHIP, although these features do not appear in the form
of the word itself. Only if we reproduce them as in *Lebenspartner, Ehepartner,*
or *der Partner* (with the definite article implying the relevant features) does our
translation have the necessary degree of precision.

In the same text illnesses are mentioned as a consequence of stress:

> (6)Stress, indeed, has been linked with conditions like migraine, asthma and ul-
> cers. *(The Sunday Times Magazine,* May 28, 1978)

Here, similarly, we cannot translate *ulcer* by *Geschwür* only. Within the context
of illnesses caused by stress, the feature IN THE STOMACH is activated by the
reader, although this feature is not specified in the form of the word itself. A
sufficiently precise translation in this context is *Magengeschwür.* Both examples
illustrate the foregrounding of semantic features in the process of comprehension
and translation.

We have not discussed the translation of technical vocabulary so far. Is
semantic analysis, in the way I have presented it, also relevant for this field?
There is a widespread opinion that technical translation is less complicated as far
as semantics is concerned, because the meanings of words are precisely defined
and terminologies are standardized. The works of Arntz (1986), Arntz&Picht
(1989) and Schmitt (1985,1986,1992) have shown that things are not that
simple, and that the semantic precision of technical terms is very often a fiction.

Schmitt has shown that there are cases where technical terms are
"imprecise", and that this "imprecision" can be explained situationally or con-
textually. Technical texts must thus be seen within the same pragmatic frame-

work as any text dealing with non-technical topics. They are also determined by situational constraints which may lead to the same psycholinguistic semantic considerations as those described so far. There is an example given by Schmitt (1986). In injection moulding, there is a terminological distinction between *closing force* (the relatively low force needed for closing the two halves of the tool) and *clamping force* (the relatively strong force needed for keeping the tool closed against the very high pressure of the injection process). The German terminological equivalent for the first term is *Schließkraft*, and for the latter *Zuhaltekraft*. What is interesting to note from a pragmatic point of view is that in the language used on the shop floor (the PROVINCE-dimension, cf. Chapter 3, section 3.1), in spite of lack of terminological clarity, *Schließkraft* and not *Zuhaltekraft* is used as an equivalent for *clamping force*. Nevertheless, there are no comprehension problems. In more scientific texts, however, we normally find *Zuhaltekraft* (cf. Schmitt 1986:271ff.).

Just as in the case of *bedroom, greenfly,* etc. the distinctive feature is lexicalized in the very form of the English word, but under certain pragmatic conditions it is suppressed in translation; in the case of *Schließkraft* it is indeed replaced by another "incorrect" feature, which is in turn suppressed by the situational conditions in which the term is used, and by this process of suppression the correct understanding is achieved.

There is another example given by Schmitt (1985) which shows that the use of technical terms may even have cultural motivations. In American English, instead of the generic term *generator* we often find the subordinate term *alternator*. The reason is a cultural one. In the United States the alternator has been part of the standard equipment of cars for a much longer time than in Europe. In British English texts, however, we often find *dynamo* instead of *generator*, because in Great Britain until the end of the nineteen seventies these machines produced direct and not alternating current (cf. Schmitt 1985:2). This phenomenon is very much in line with Fillmore's idea of comprehension. It could be argued that in car technology in the United States and in Britain two different cultural scenes or rather scenarios in the sense of higher-order structures (cf. Bobrow 1975:23.) have developed which have subsequently led to different frames.

When they have to be translated into German as specific terms these words produce no semantic disturbances. *Alternator* can be translated by its semantic equivalent *Drehstromgenerator,* and *dynamo* by its equivalent *Gleichstromgenerator.*

It is in their function as generic terms that we must be aware of their cultural implications. Both American English *alternator* and British English *dynamo* then have to be rendered by a generic term in German. It is interesting to note that situational constraints similar to those observable in the translation of *clamping force* and *closing force* come into play here as well. In manuals, *alternator* and *dynamo* are conventionally translated by *Generator*, in workshop language the word used in German is *Lichtmaschine*.

Semantically speaking, there is no direct equivalence but a suppression of semantic features when *alternator* and *dynamo* are translated in their function as generic terms, although in these cases the semantic features are not lexicalized in the very forms of the words as in *bedroom, Roman Catholic,* etc.

4.4 "Lexical gaps" and how to fill them

There is another phenomenon which continually seems to attract the interest of semanticians and translation theoreticians alike. There may be a word in one language for which there does not seem to be a counterpart in another language at all, and for anyone who sticks to the word as the ultimate unit of translation this is a problem indeed. Here is a typical example. There was a report in the *Sunday Times* about recent findings in the treatment of diabetes and high blood-pressure. It had been observed that a diet of porridge helped to regulate blood sugar and fats. Oats apparently contain a gummy fibre material which reduces cholesterol and also blood sugar. There have also been experiments with wheat bran and beans:

> (7a) They (the patients) improved but Anderson found it was not the wheat bran but beans which were responsible. Beans, particularly haricot and kidney, contain complex carbohydrate which acts in a similar way to oat gum.
> (*The Sunday Times*, September 20, 1981)

The problem here is how to translate *haricot* and *kidney*. In *The Dictionary of Contemporary English* they are defined as *"haricot* any of several types of small white bean, *kidney* a type of bean that is shaped like a kidney and eaten as a vegetable".* Both words, obviously, are hyponyms of *bean* insofar as they contain the additional feature that the seeds are eaten and not the pods. They differ, it seems, as to the size and form of the seeds. Are there equivalent words in German?

The information given in bilingual dictionaries is rather confusing. *Collins English-German Dictionary* offers "Gartenbohne" for both words. *Langenscheidts Großes Schulwörterbuch* has "weiße Bohne" for "haricot bean" and "(Vits/ Schmink-) Bohne" for "kidney bean". In *Duden-Oxford Großwörterbuch Englisch* we find "grüne Bohne" and "weiße Bohne" for "haricot bean", and "Gartenbohne" for "kidney bean". In *Langenscheidt's Encyclopaedic Dictionary* we find "Garten- Schminkbohne (Phaseolus vulgaris)" for "haricot bean" and "1. weiße Bohne 2. Feuerbohne (Phaseolus coccineus)" for "kidney bean". This is contradictory and confusing. Apparently, it is not clear at all what the distinction is between the two words. Further, there seem to be difficulties in finding two equivalent German terms. It looks as if we are here faced with a "lexical gap". There is the generic term (hyperonym) *Bohne* in German and the specific term (hyponym) *weiße Bohne,* the latter implying that the seeds are eaten, but there seem to be no further terms for distinguishing types of beanseeds as to their size and form.

Lexical gaps can usually be filled by paraphrases. How precise do we have to be though? If we apply the *maxim of the functionally necessary degree of precision* there should not be any serious problems. In the example quoted it is important to know that beans, apart from oats, contain that gummy substance which reduces blood sugar, and this substance is part of the seeds of beans, as anyone knows who has ever cooked white beans. The semantic feature SEED must therefore be reproduced in the translation, and if our translation has the same function as the original, that is, informing a large number of readers about new findings in the field of medicine, it is precise enough to write

> (7b) Bohnen, vor allem Bohnenkerne/vor allem weiße Bohnen, enthalten komplexe Kohlehydrate...

If our translation has a function that differs from the original we might have to be more precise. Suppose we had to translate the same text for doctors working in a clinic for diabetics, then they would want to know which kinds of beanseeds should be used for a diet. We would then have to reproduce the features that distinguish *haricot* from *kidney,* and our translation could read:

> (7c) Bohnen, vor allem weiße Bohnen und Feuerbohnenkerne...

Recently the word *Kidney-Bohnen* has appeared on tins in German shops, and we could therefore also translate

> (7d) Bohnen, vor allem kleine weiße Bohnen und Kidney-Bohnen...

If our translation, to mention a third and final function, is supposed to be read by gardeners who grow beans for those clinics, one would be justified in using the technical terms given in *Langenscheidt's Encyclopaedic Dictionary,* and our translation could then be

> (7e) Bohnen, vor allem Phaseolus vulgaris und Phaseolus coccineus...

The technical terms would be the appropriate equivalents in this case.

Our example (7a) had a medical touch and to a certain extent it contained special vocabulary. It is a commonplace that in bilingual or multilingual terminologies of all fields lexical gaps provide a major problem (cf. Arntz/Picht 1989:170ff.) Terminologists have developed guidelines on how to fill these gaps (cf. Arntz 1986:301ff., Arntz/Picht 1989:190ff.) I shall not go into detail here, but I would like to stress one point, which has become obvious in our discussion of technical terms but which seems sometimes to be neglected by terminologists. Our decisions on how to fill terminological gaps should be governed by functional considerations. Let us take the much quoted distinction between *solicitor* and *barrister*, for example. If we look up *solicitor* in *Duden-Oxford Groß- wörterbuch Englisch* we find:

> *(Brit.: lawyer) Rechtsanwalt, der/ -anwältin, die (der/die nicht vor höheren Gerichten auftritt).*

For *barrister* we find:

> a) *(Brit.)* Barrister, *der*; Rechtsanwalt/-anwältin vor höheren Gerichten, *der*; b) *(Amer. lawyer)* Rechtsanwalt, *der/* -anwältin, *die.*

In order to fill the lexical gaps in German, the dictionary typically resorts to definitions, and the user thus gets to know the distinction between the two words. What is a translator supposed to do? Does he/she have to include the definitions in his/her translation? It all depends on the function of the word within a text. If *solicitor*, say, appears in the general context of a novel it may be precise enough to translate *Rechtsanwalt/anwältin*. If, however, the word is part of a text describing professional training in Great Britain, an additional piece of information, such as given in the dictionary, should be added.

4.5 Teaching meaning, comprehension and translation

In the first chapter when analysing the TAPs, we saw that students had problems with understanding words in texts. Often a proper balance between top-down and bottom-up processes was lacking. This became evident, for instance, in their fear of interferences, in faulty one-to-one correspondences, in their misuse of world knowledge and in their attitude toward paraphrasing.

By offering models such as the ones presented in this chapter we can help our students to rationalize their comprehension and translation processes, so that these might become more successful. One of the main insights which have evolved from our discussion of semantic translation problems is that *successful translation is often nothing else but the verbalization of our comprehension*. I have tried to combine psycholinguistic models with more traditional approaches, and I would suggest that the two main principles which have emerged from this combination are *foregrounding and suppression of semantic features*. This also means that comprehension and translation is not a static but a *dynamic process*.

In adjusting our semantic decisions to the comprehension process and to the function of the passage in question or of the overall translation we should always be able to show where the boundaries are within which our solutions will have to be found. In other words, we should always be able to decide on the *sufficient degree of semantic precision*. By applying this method we should find it easier to argue for or against specific solutions, when discussing semantic problems with our students.

In the course of this we will also be able to supply our students with arguments which they can use later on in their professional life. It is a common experience for translators that the people who commission translations are often very naive linguistically, and they find fault with a translation when they notice that a word of the original text does not turn up. With professional arguments at their disposal, translators will, it is hoped, find it easier to convince these people.

As for the marking of translations, the application of our method might well mean that we would have to cast aside long-used criteria. It is very likely that traditionally-minded teachers of translation courses when faced with translations such as (7b) will object: "The student has been imprecise. There is a word missing here! The student doesn't seem to know the difference between those two English words. This ought to be marked as a mistake!" Such verdicts should be met with the reply, "You are isolating the words from their contexts, and as a result you are thus losing sight of the function of your translation. The main thing asked of a translation is that it should fulfil the function chosen for it in the best possible way. All details concerning the translation of individual words ought to be subordinated to this end." We shall deal with the evaluation of translations and the marking of errors more extensively in Chapter 6.

Chapter 5

Text analysis and the use of dictionaries

5.1 Harmony between monolingual dictionaries and context

The analysis of word meaning, as we have seen in the preceding chapter, involves two complementary processes. When analysing the source text we are trying to get an idea of the meaning potential of a given word, and at the same time we examine how, as an interplay of bottom-up and top-down processes, this meaning potential is activated by the context in which the word is used. In our production of the target text we search for the words which have the meaning we want to express, and we make sure that these words fit into the context, in other words, that our intended meaning is activated by the interplay of potential word meaning and context determination. If the lexical knowledge we need to perform these processes is insufficient, then dictionaries can inform us about the meaning potential of words.

Ideally, there is harmony between meaning potential described in dictionaries and context. As for the source text, harmony is achieved if the definitions found in monolingual dictionaries fit into the context. This can be tested by substituting the definitions for the words in question. As for the target text, harmony is achieved if the equivalents found in bilingual dictionaries can be used within their target context to activate the meaning we want to express.

We shall begin with such cases of harmony, especially as far as monolingual dictionaries are concerned, and shall then gradually turn to cases where there are discrepancies between the information found in dictionaries and the use of words in a given text. We shall be concerned with techniques of dictionary use, which involve skills in finding the relevant meaning of polysemous words, in interpreting definitions, examples, contextual clues, collocators and phrases. In a special section stylistic labels will be dealt with. Apart from discussing how to read dictionary entries I shall also present text-linguistic models for inferring meaning from context.

I shall point out some basic differences between bilingual and monolingual dictionaries. I shall be mainly concerned, however, with monolingual dictionaries, for reasons that will become apparent when interpreting the examples.

I shall not deal with "simple" cases, as when the meaning of a source language word is completely clear and our only problem is that we do not know, or cannot for the moment think of, a target language equivalent, and the information in bilingual dictionaries is such that we can easily choose a correct target word. Such a case would be the translation of *talk* in a sentence like:

> Tom could already talk at the age of one year.

In *PONS GLOBALWÖRTERBUCH (englisch-deutsch)*, London: Collins 1983, we find the information:

> **talk** vi 1. sprechen... (have conversation also) sich unterhalten, (*bird, doll, child*) sprechen...

Without more ado we could translate:

> Tom konnte bereits im Alter von einem Jahr sprechen.

Rather I shall try to show what we can do with dictionaries in more problematic cases where we must make use of text-linguistic models in order to complement the information gained from the dictionaries. It may be a commonplace, and at the risk of repeating myself, I would want to stress the need to make it clear to our students that words are not isolated units but should be seen as embedded in a text. It is an experience familiar to us all that students, especially early on in their undergraduate career, naively stick to words, and when arguing about translations, make statements like "That's the word I found in the dictionary."

We should show our students that dictionaries have limitations, we should tell them that they must not expect too much of a dictionary, and we should teach them techniques of analysing the context in order to supplement their dictionary research techniques. These techniques are especially useful, as I shall show below, in cases where there is a discrepancy between the information given by the dictionary and the context which is relevant for the word in question.

Let us begin with cases where there is harmony. Some years ago there was an article in *The Sunday Times Magazine* about "talking" chimpanzees:

> Moja, together with a dozen or so other chimps and one gorilla in the United States, talks. She doesn't *speak* - she talks. She communicates with her fingers in American Sign Language, devised for, and used by, hundreds of thousands of deaf Americans. At the moment she has a vocabulary of more than 150 "words" (that is, signs).
>
> (*The Sunday Times Magazine*, November 18, 1979)

The words which present a problem here, especially when using bilingual dictionaries, are *speak* and *talk*. The quotations are from two dictionaries which have been recommended to our students because they are based on modern lexicographical principles and give contextual clues for the various meanings of polysemous words. For our purposes, only the intransitive uses of the words are quoted. The following equivalents are offered by *PONS GLOBALWÖRTER-BUCH*:

speak ... vi 1. (*talk, be on talking terms*) sprechen, reden..., (*converse*) reden, sich unterhalten 2. (*make a speech*) reden..., sprechen
talk vi 1. sprechen... (have conversation also) sich unterhalten, (*bird, doll, child*) sprechen... 2. (*mention*) sprechen, reden...3.(*chatter*) reden, schwatzen... 4.(*gossip*) reden, klatschen... 5. (*reveal secret*) reden...
PONS GLOBALWÖRTERBUCH (englisch-deutsch), London: Collins 1983

In DUDEN OXFORD we find

speak 1. v.i. a) sprechen.....2. v.t. a) (*utter*) sprechen (Satz, Wort, Sprache)...b) (*make known*) sagen (Wahrheit)
talk v.i. a) (*speak*) sprechen, reden (**with, to** mit); (*lecture*) sprechen; (*converse*) sich unterhalten; (*have talks*) Gespräche führen; (*gossip*) reden...b) (*have the power of speech*) sprechen; **animals don't talk**: Tiere können nicht sprechen; c) (*betray secrets*) reden;... (*DUDEN OXFORD Großwörterbuch Englisch*, Mannheim: Duden Verlag 1990)

By offering indicators in brackets for the various meanings of the words both dictionaries give us a very detailed idea of the semantic structure of the headwords. But no meaning can be found that fits into our text. In fact, by mentioning the phrase *animals don't talk* and its translation "Tiere können nicht sprechen", the *Duden Oxford* may lead us to the conclusion that *talk* in our text is used in a rather strange, perhaps unidiomatic way.

If we just use the German equivalents offered, it proves hard to express the contrast obvious in our text between spoken language and sign language. Depending on which dictionary or which combinations we prefer, we might arrive at translations such as:

- Sie spricht nicht - sie redet
- Sie redet nicht - sie spricht.
- Sie unterhält sich nicht - sie redet.
- Sie redet nicht - sie unterhält sich.

These sentences, of course, do express oppositions, but not the one meant in our text.

If I am dealing with the use of bilingual dictionaries in some detail, it is because our findings here are typical. Bilingual dictionaries by their very nature cannot help us with problems such as these. As they have to offer target language equivalents on the word level their underlying semantic structure is strongly influenced by the target language system. In our case, there are no single words in German by which the contrast of meaning present in our text could be expressed, and therefore the contrast between *speak* and *talk* in our text is not mentioned, in fact cannot be mentioned, in bilingual English-German dictionaries.

It could be argued that we do not need any dictionary at all for analysing the meaning of *speak* and *talk* in our text, because the context makes their meaning clear enough. This is certainly true for our example, but we have all come across words the meaning of which we cannot guess from their context, a situation which, indeed, always occurs when words carry new as opposed to given information. In those cases we may have to turn to dictionaries for help. I shall therefore make use of our example to point out some basic differences between bilingual and monolingual dictionaries and demonstrate how we can extract information from the entries in monolingual ones.

Monolingual dictionaries are more helpful in analysing source text words, because they define meaning within one language system. If we compare the definitions relevant in our text given under the headings *speak* and *talk* in a number of monolingual English dictionaries it seems at first glance, however, as if the words have synonymous meanings:

> **speak** to express thoughts aloud, using the voice; talk
> **talk** to use or produce words; speak
> *Dictionary of Contemporary English*, London & Berlin: Langenscheidt-Longman 1987 (DCE)

> **speak** to make (verbal utterances); utter (words)
> **talk** to express one's thoughts, feelings or desires by means of words (to), speak (to)
> Collins Dictionary of the English Language , London & Glasgow: Collins 1979 (CED)

> **speak** When you **speak,** you use your voice in order to say words
> **talk** If you can **talk**, you have the ability to use spoken words to express your thoughts, ideas or feelings
> Collins-COBUILD English Language Dictionary, London and Glasgow: Collins 1987

> **speak** make articulate verbal utterances in an ordinary (not singing) voice
> **talk** converse or communicate ideas by spoken words
> The Concise Oxford Dictionary of Current English, Oxford: Clarendon 1990 (COD)

The DCE mutually uses *speak* and *talk* to explain each other. The CED uses *speak* to explain *talk*. The definitions in Collins COBUILD and in the COD resemble each other insofar as they both refer to speech ("use your voice in order to say words", "use spoken words", "articulate verbal utterances", "spoken words").

On closer examination, however, we can observe different specifications for *speak* and *talk*. In the definition of *speak* in the DCE we find "use the voice", but this specification does not appear in the DCE for *talk*. In the CED, for *speak* there is the specification "verbal utterance", which does not appear in its definition of *talk*. In Collins-COBUILD in the definition of *speak* we may interpret "you use your voice", and in the COD, under *speak* we may interpret "ordinary voice" as a similar specification. One may draw the conclusion that *speak* compared with *talk* has the additional semantic feature "using speech-organs". We would then have a hyponymy relation between the two words, with *talk* being the superordinate or generic term and *speak* the or specific term, e.g.

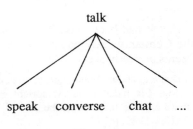

Figure 1

This interpretation makes sense in our text, because Moja the chimpanzee cannot utter words using her speech organs. Our hypothesis is further supported by the fact that *talk,* among many other meanings (there are 12 meanings listed in the DCE, for example), has one that fits our text exactly. Under number 2 in the DCE this is defined as:

> to express thoughts as if by speech: People who cannot speak or hear can talk by using signs.

Both the definition and the example fit into our context. The same is true for definition 2 under *talk* in the CED:

> to communicate or exchange thoughts by other means: *lovers talk with their eyes*

Collins-COBUILD and the COD, however, have no comparable definitions under *talk*. It has become obvious from our example, among other things, that polysemy is the normal type of relation between a lexical item and its meanings. This is one of the first facts we should make our students aware of, and when doing this we should also tell them, as the missing definitions in Collins-Cobuild and in the COD show, that not all the meanings of words will be found in dictionaries.

When using monolingual dictionaries, we first of all select the meaning which fits the given context. We then recognize the relevant semantic features, a distinctive feature in the case of *speak* and *talk,* in the definitions and in the examples provided, and we then try to reproduce this feature in the target language.

The explanatory material in monolingual dictionaries may actually be helpful in stimulating a translation. When translating this text with my students in class the example in the DCE *People who cannot speak or hear can talk by using signs* immediately brought forth "kommunizieren" from one of my students - a fully acceptable solution:

> (a) Sie spricht nicht - sie kommuniziert, und zwar in der Amerikanischen Zeichensprache.

A few months after it had been published in England a translation of the article appeared in the German weekly paper *Zeitmagazin* with another variant for *talk,* which also seems perfectly acceptable:

> (b) Wie etwa ein Dutzend andere Schimpansen und ein Gorilla in den Vereinigten Staaten spricht Moja. Sie redet nicht; sie spricht eine unhörbare Sprache. Sie gebraucht die Amerikanische Zeichensprache...
> (*Zeitmagazin* 17, 18.4.1980, p.17.)

From the point of view of creativity, to take up the topic of Chapter 2 on this occasion, these translations can be regarded as creative solutions. There is no formal equivalence between source and target text, and one may say that they have been brought about by the ability of finding synonyms, which again is a sign of divergent thinking.

What is striking here is that (a) has "Sie spricht nicht", whereas (b) says "Sie spricht". The explanation is that "spricht" in "sie spricht eine unhörbare Sprache" takes on a new meaning in which the use of spoken words is suppressed.

When teaching translation, we should practice the techniques of using a dictionary. The discussion of the example made it clear, I think, that a basic knowledge of semantics might be very useful, especially the basic concepts and methods of structural semantics, for instance polysemy, synonymy, hyponymy and semantic feature analysis, for these are the main concepts and methods that have gone into making dictionaries until now.

I have been talking about the use of monolingual English dictionaries from the point of view of translating into German as one's mother tongue, and it might be argued that we need a native speaker's competence to arrive at such translations as the ones quoted. What ways are there to produce these kinds of translations if our knowledge of the target language is not that perfect?

Definitions and examples in monolingual dictionaries, as we have seen, can stimulate translations. What happens, in fact, is that the words of the source text are paraphrased by the material in the dictionaries, and paraphrasing is exactly one of the most basic techniques in translation, as we have seen in many instances. Krings and Lörscher, who analysed TAPs of translations into the foreign language, observed that intralingual paraphrasing was one of the most frequent means of finding interlingual equivalents (cf. section 1.3.6 of this book). I would imagine, for instance, that the definition in the CED mentioned above ("to communicate or exchange thoughts by other means") could easily lead to the adequate German translation "kommunizieren". And if the translator was not sure whether English *communicate* could actually be translated by a German formally very similar word he should, with the paraphrase as a source text starting point, have no problems in finding an answer in a bilingual English-German dictionary or a monolingual German dictionary. *PONS Global-wörterbuch*, for instance, offers:

> **communicate**... 2. (convey or exchange thoughts) sich verständigen, kommunizieren...

Kommunizieren thus appears to be an adequate solution, and what is even more interesting is that by the use of *communicate* as a point of departure for our search, we also arrive at *sich verständigen,* an equivalent which was not mentioned in bilingual dictionaries under *talk,* but which in our text is an excellent translation as well.

In Duden. *Das große Wörterbuch der deutschen Sprache*, Mannheim 1978 we find

> **kommunizieren** ...2. *sich verständigen, miteinander sprechen*: Diese Jungen nehmen...die Gelegenheit wahr, mit einem Menschen, der sich ihnen intensiv zuwendet, zu k. (Schmidt, Strichjungengespräche 167); wie differenziert man demzufolge über einzelne Schneearten kommuniziert (Sprachpflege 10, 1974, 209)

Here again, *kommunizieren* is defined in a way which shows that it can serve as a translation, and *sich verständigen* is also mentioned as a paraphrase. Thus the monolingual *Duden* also proves to be a means of finding additional translations.

From the examples in *Duden* one might, however, draw the conclusion that *kommunizieren* involves a direct or indirect object, either in the form of a partner or a topic. I think, this is an instance where it becomes clear that one must not overinterpret examples. Sentences without an object such as *Er/sie kann gut kommunizieren* are perfectly acceptable in German. Moreover, one might argue that the types of objects which appear in the *Duden* examples are implied in our text, since Moja "talks" with human researchers, and when she "talks" to them a topic or message is logically implied.

5.2 Problems with examples

The examples quoted for *speak* and *talk* in the monolingual English dictionaries consulted were in semantic accordance with the definitions. Sometimes, however, there are discrepancies. Here is a typical example. In English academic writing, statements are often introduced by *suggest* as in the following text on the connection between puberty and intellectual development:

> The Stanford scientists are still seeking reasons for the connections between maturity and intelligence, but some researchers suggest it has to do with the "lateralization" of the brain.
> *(Newsweek, March 1, 1982)*

Among the definitions offered in monolingual dictionaries of the polysemous word *suggest* we find the ones that fit into our context:

- say or write (an idea to be considered) (DCE)
- to put forward for consideration (CED)
- propose (a theory, plan, or hypothesis) (COD)
- put forward for consideration (*Oxford Advanced Learner's Dictionary of Current English*. London: Oxford University Press 1974, ALD)
- If you suggest something to someone, you say something to them which then puts an idea into their mind *(Collins COBUILD. English Language Dictionary*. London & Glasgow 1987)
- to offer for consideration or as a hypothesis (Webster's Seventh New Collegiate Dictionary. Springfield, Mass. 1970)

The definitions are helpful; most of the examples, however, as we shall see, are misleading. If we use them to trigger translations, we will be led to incorrect solutions. Thus, if we read the examples

> I'd like to suggest an alternative plan. I suggest leaving now/that we leave now. Can you suggest how we should do it? (DCE)
> I suggest Smith for the post (CED)
> I suggested a visit. I suggest going to the theatre. What did you suggest to the manager? (ALD)

with a view to translating *suggest* into German, we will immediately think of *vorschlagen,* a word which does not make sense in our text. Only in *Collins COBUILD* do we find examples which might point to appropriate translations:

> I'm not suggesting that the accident was your fault... It would be foolish to suggest that everyone in Britain was rich...*(Collins COBUILD).*

Scrutiny of these examples may prompt translations like "der Meinung sein", "behaupten" both of which fit well with our text. The weakness of the entries in the other dictionaries lies in their limited scope. Their definitions are comprehensive enough but their examples are not, because they do not take account of the fact that *suggest* in its function of a performative verb (verb referring to the speech act being performed) is polysemous. It can both refer to a directive speech act, i.e. an attempt by the speaker to get the hearer to do something (cf. Searle 1976:11), which is implied in the examples in the DCE, CED and ALD, and it can refer to a representative speech act, i.e. a commitment - in our case a very cautious one - of the speaker to something being the case (cf. Searle 1976:10), and this meaning is implied only in the COBUILD examples.

What consequences can be drawn from this state of affairs for the teaching of translation? Dictionary users should learn to be cautious and critical. They should reckon with the fact that examples will not always fulfil their role of triggering translations. In my experience, dictionaries are often imprecise when explaining illocutions, not only when describing the meaning of performative verbs - of which, according to Austin (1962:150), there are around 5,000 in English - but also when explaining other linguistic forms which serve as illocutionary force indicators, like sentence adverbials such as *now, in fact, actually, indeed* etc. (cf. Kussmaul 1978).

In all those cases we must learn to apply techniques of analysing the context in order to supplement the information gained from dictionaries. When analysing the meaning of performative verbs it may be helpful to look at the propositional content of the sentence. The proposition, for instance, of the sentence subordinate to *suggest* in our example, is not a future action of the hearer, which would fit in with *suggest* in its meaning of *vorschlagen,* but a discovery made by the speaker, and this type of proposition can be introduced by verbs which are semantically related to English *state, maintain* or German *feststellen, behaupten.*

The speech act model may perhaps sound too complicated to some of us for teaching purposes. For a simpler method the concept of collocation might be used. In the case of performative verbs there would then be collocation between the verb in the main clause and the content of the subordinate clause.

Finally, for a precise translation of our example I would suggest:

...aber einige Wissenschaftler stellten die These auf, dies habe etwas mit der Lateralization des Gehirns zu tun.

For problems occurring with collocations, especially when translating into the foreign language, we can, of course, always make use of the examples in monolingual and, if we are lucky enough to find them, also in bilingual dictionaries. If we want to find out, taking up an example quoted earlier (section 1.2.1), whether *Phase* or *Periode* collocates with *Schlaf* and if we consult *Duden, Das große Wörterbuch der deutschen Sprache,* for instance, under the headword *Schlaf,* we will find that *Schlaf* and *Phase* even form a compound in German: "Schlafphase, die (Fachspr.)".

In addition, there are special dictionaries of idiomatic usage. But these dictionaries are usually not comprehensive as far as collocations are concerned. Ideally, we should have collocational dictionaries (cf. van der Wouden, 1992) Some work has been done on collocation types for Russian and French (cf. Mel'cuk / Zolkovsky 1984, Mel'cuk et al. 1984), and there is *The BBI Combinatory Dictionary of English* published by Benjamins, Amsterdam 1986.

5.3 Dictionary versus context

In the previous section we were considering cases where dictionaries provide appropriate definitions but where the examples provided are problematic. Even more critical situations arise, however, when dictionaries fail even to provide an appropriate definition of words occurring in the text to be translated. Here is a case in point.

Willem van der Eyken in the first Chapter of his book *Pre-School Years* observes that education in the second half of the twentieth century is becoming more and more important. He writes:

> But this new recognition is also accompanied by an extraordinarily vague view of the ultimate purpose of education, quite unlike the hard, practical approach of many earlier cultures. The Greeks wanted to produce philosophers, and directed their education towards that end. The Romans sought to train members of the senate. The early church provided education as a training for the clergy. The British education system of the nineteenth century was aimed at producing legislators and colonial administrators. Those who devised these education systems knew what they wanted, and saw to it that they produced the right results. By contrast, a country like England, which this year will spend more than 2500 million pounds, or 6 percent of its national income, on education, has only just begun to question whether the subjects that are taught in school are the right ones, and whether the ways in which knowledge is transmitted are the most efficient.
> (Willem van der Eyken, *Pre-School Years*, Harmondsworth: Penguin Books 1967:13)

One of the problems is how to translate *hard* (line 3). German translators will have *hart, schwierig, schwer* stored in their memories. These equivalents, however, do not make much sense in our text. We may conclude that *hard* must have an additional meaning. In four of the dictionaries consulted, however, no meaning can be found which fits into our text. Only *Webster's* offers a definition (under number 7a) which might make sense:

free from sentimentality or illusion: REALISTIC (good hard sense)

The example going with the definition (*good hard sense*), however, is too short to be helpful. In the DCE, on the other hand, under number 11, one of the examples proves to be more useful for our purposes than the definition:

> based on what is clearly true or can be proved: *The police have several theories about the case, but no hard evidence. Can linguistics ever be **a hard science** like physics?*

Hard science might trigger off German *empirisch,* which fits in with the examples following in our text where the vocationally-oriented educational aims of the Greeks, Romans, the early church etc. are mentioned. In the event of the dictionary we use not providing us with a suitable definition or example, this part of the text will help us to infer the meaning of *hard,* so that we might - by means of creative divergent thinking - also translate it by *realitätsbezogen* or *wirklichkeitsnah.* What we have been doing here is tracing the interaction of a frame in Fillmore's terms (i.e. *hard* and its potential meaning) with a scene (i.e. the description of education in earlier cultures) in order to activate the meaning of a word.

There is a more specific text-analytical model for describing the unfolding of meaning in texts. Presentation of information in cohesive, i.e. well-structured, texts is governed by communicative principles where the relationship between new information and information already given or implied plays an important role. This model is usually referred to as *functional sentence perspective* or *theme-rheme arrangement* (= the arrangement between given and new information) (cf. Danes 1978). It has been repeatedly made use of in translation studies (cf. Hönig/Kussmaul 1982:110, Gerzymisch-Arbogast 1986, Hatim/Mason 1990:209ff.) Following Danes, we might say that in our text there is a progression of themes derived from a hyper-theme. The hyper-theme is *many earlier cultures,* and derived themes are *the Greeks, the Romans* etc.

hyper-theme: *many earlier cultures*

        derived themes:
        the Greeks
        the Romans
        the early church
        the British education system

Figure 2

In addition, there is a type of progression, which has not been discussed in the literature so far, of hyper-rheme and derived rhemes. In our example, *hard, practical approach* is the hyper-rheme, and *produce philosophers, train members of the senate, training for the clergy* etc. are the derived rhemes.

hyper-rheme: *hard, practical approach*

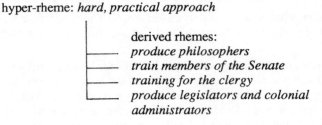

derived rhemes:
produce philosophers
train members of the Senate
training for the clergy
produce legislators and colonial administrators

Figure 3

It is from the derived rhemes that the meaning of the hyper-rheme can be inferred. I would recommend *theme and rheme progression* as models for rationalizing our analyses of word meanings in contexts.

In the preceding examples, dictionary information could be used, to some extent and with some reservations, for meaning analysis. We may come across cases where this is no longer possible and where we have to rely on text analysis alone. The following passage is taken from the introduction to a book on the sociology of religion:

> Sociology is essentially a way of looking at things. It assumes not so much a posture as a stance. It should not - and usually does not - pretend to be a predictive science, but it can claim to provide new perspectives in the study of familiar subjects. This is particularly true in sociological analyses of religion.
> (Eric Carlton. *Patterns of Belief: Religions in Society.* London 1973: 11.)

Posture and *stance* (line 2) are used antithetically here. What information is offered in dictionaries? The figurative meaning of *posture* relevant in our sentence is defined as:

- a way of behaving or thinking on a particular occasion; ATTITUDE: The government's posture on this new trade agreement seems very unhelpful (DCE)
- mental attitude, frame of mind (CED)
- a mental or spiritual attitude or condition (COD)
- frame of mind, attitude: Will the government alter its posture over aid to the railways? (ALD)
- an attitude that you have towards a particular subject, situation, or problem, e.g. *They are trying to adopt a more co-operative posture.* (Collins

COBUILD)
- frame of mind, attitude (Webster's).

Stance is defined as:
- a way of thinking, esp. a publicly stated position regarding a particular situation; ATTITUDE: What's your government's stance on nuclear disarmament? The president has adopted a stance on terrorism. (DCE)
- general emotional or intellectual attitude: *a leftist stance* (CED)
- a standpoint; an attitude of mind (COD)
- person's intellectual attitude (ALD)
- your attitude about a particular matter. They criticized Martin Luther King for his rigid stance on non-violence ... The newspaper defended its unpopular editorial stance. (Collins COBUILD)
- intellectual or emotional attitude (Webster's)

Even if we try hard, we cannot infer any meaning distinctions between *posture* and *stance* from the definitions given in the dictionaries. The same term, *attitude,* appears in the definitions of both words, either when explaining it by a synonym or when placing the word within a known class (e.g."mental attitude" CED). In addition, we find synonymous terms ("mental"/"mind", "intellectual") when identifying the words within a known class (e.g. for *posture*: "mental attitude" CED, for *stance*: "intellectual attitude" CED).

In our text, however, there is a contrast between *posture* and *stance*. In other words, there must be a distinctive feature that is activated by the context. Looking at thematic progression we find that there is a continuous theme. The text starts with *sociology* which is then being referred to by the pronoun *it.* More relevant, here again, is rhematic progression. The rheme of the first sentence (*a way of looking at things*) is made more specific in the next sentences (*not so much a posture as a stance...it does not pretend to be a predictive science, but it can claim to provide new perspectives*), and this specification is achieved by means of contrasting concepts.

hyper-rheme: a way of looking at things

derived rhemes:
not so much a posture as a stance
not...a predictive science, but... provide new perspectives

Figure 4

The result is an affinity in meaning between *posture* and *predictive science* on the one hand and between *stance* and *new perspectives* on the other. With a little bit of ingenuity we can assign the feature "rigid" to *posture* and "flexible" to *stance*.

This seems to contradict the information presented in our dictionaries. According to the example in Collins COBUILD "rigid" appears to collocate with *stance,* and according to the example in the ALD flexibility seems to be a feature of *posture*. There are two ways of explaining this contradiction. One could either say that the use of the words in our text is idiosyncratic or one could try to find additional information in the dictionaries. It could, in fact, be argued that the non-figurative meaning of the words may have influenced their use in our text. In the DCE, for instance, we find:

> **posture** 1...the general way of holding the body, esp. the back, shoulders, and head when standing, walking, and sitting. Humans have a naturally erect posture. good/ bad posture
> **stance** 1...a way of standing, esp. when getting ready to hit the ball in various sports: *First take up the correct stance.*

When referring to visible actions *posture* could be said to have the feature "permanent" and *stance* could be said to have the feature "occasional". The words would thus be used metaphorically in our text.

Be that as it may, it has become evident, I think, that there are cases where textual analysis is a safer and more economical way of solving semantic problems than looking up words in dictionaries. We may recall the role semantic features play in the process of comprehension, described in the preceding chapter. Features, we said, are being foregrounded or suppressed. We might say that in the case of *posture* and *stance*, the features "permanent" and "occasional" are being foregrounded by the use of the word in this specific context. For a translation I would suggest:

> Die Soziologie ist im Grunde nichts anderes als eine Art, die Dinge zu sehen. Sie vertritt dabei weniger eine feste Position, sondern vermittelt eher eine Einstellung. Sie sollte nicht den Anspruch erheben - und normalerweise tut sie es auch nicht - eine Wissenschaft im strengen Sinne zu sein, die in der Lage ist, Gesetze zu formulieren, sie kann aber von sich behaupten, daß sie neue Perspektiven bei der Untersuchung bekannter Themen eröffnet...

The semantic feature "permanent", obviously, is rendered in "feste Position". One may ask, where the feature "occasional" appears in the translation. It is implied in "Einstellung". It could, of course be made explicit by translating "flexible Einstellung", but I do not think this is necessary.

5.4 Unusual use

I have hinted at the possibility that a writer's use of words might be idiosyncratic and not in accordance with general semantic usage. If this happens, dictionaries will not be able to help us any more as, for instance, in the following passage:

> In fact, allergy or intolerance to environmental substances is no new thing and has probably always been a by-product of man's evolution in a changing world. The word ecology was first used in 1866 to refer to the mutual relations of living things to their physical surroundings and to each other, as described by Darwin. Implicit in the concept of ecological balance is the long and intricate process of adaptation by which men come to live in harmony with their physical environment, and it is a rule of ecology that living creatures show better adaptation to those things to which they have been exposed longest: it is very much rarer to find a patient disabled by eating meat or by normal exposure to sunlight (I am not talking of sunburn), than it is to find one made ill by eating wheat or inhaling the petrochemicals in the air on a street full of heavy motor traffic.
>
> Richard Mackarness, *Not All in the Mind,* London 1976:39.

The use of *disabled* (1.13) is rather unusual. It normally refers to a visible handicap, as can be seen from the definitions given under *disable* in our dictionaries:

- ...to make (a person) unable to use his/her body properly (DCE)
- ...as by crippling (CED)
- ...(often as disabled adj.) deprive of or reduce the power to walk or do other normal activities, esp. by crippling (COD)
- ...take away the power of using the limbs (ALD)
- ...making it difficult to move about (Collins COBUILD)
- ...esp....deprive of physical strength (Webster's)

On the basis of this information the text would have a very strange meaning, namely that by eating meat or sitting in the sun it might happen, for instance, that one loses a leg or becomes paralysed - these being phenomena none too familiar to medical science.

The structuring of the text gives us some information about the intended meaning of *disable*. The words *disable* and *make ill* refer to the continuous theme of the last lines of the passage, and the words *by eating meat or by normal exposure to sunlight, by eating wheat, inhaling petrochemicals* are rhematic. The topic of these lines are illnesses which are caused by environment and food.

We talked of foregrounding of semantic features when discussing the preceding example. Here we can observe the complementary process. The feature "visible handicap" is suppressed by the context in which *disable* is used.

In addition to contextualising techniques, we might refer to our background (i.e. top-down or scenic) knowledge. We know what sort of damage is caused by these things, certainly not visible handicaps.

Obviously, *disabled* and *made ill* are used synonymously here, an unusual use, no doubt. One might consider if this is a sign of a very personal style and as such should, as a stylistic feature, be preserved in the translation. On the other hand we have here a basically informative text, and thus the most plausible rendering of denotative meaning will be our most important task.

5.5 Stylistic labels

We have discussed referential or denotative meaning so far. We may also want to get information about the connotative or stylistic meaning of words. Let us begin with an example:

> If you really want to hear about it, the first thing you'll probably want to know is where I was born, and what my lousy childhood was like, and how my parents were occupied and all before they had me, and all that David Copperfield kind of crap, but I don't feel like going into it. In the first place, that stuff bores me, and in the second place, my parents would have about two haemorrhages apiece if I told anything pretty personal about them. They're quite touchy about anything like that; especially my father. They're *nice* and all - I'm not saying that - but they're also touchy as hell. Besides, I'm not going to tell you my whole goddam autobiography or anything.
>
> (J.D. Salinger, *The Catcher in the Rye,* Harmondsworth: Penguin Books 1969:5)

One might argue that we can get an idea about the style of this passage by text analysis alone. This is true for native speakers of English. As non-native speakers of English, however, we may come across words we need for our analysis and the stylistic meaning of which is not known to us. In the same way as with the referential meaning of words we will then have to turn to dictionaries for help, and in the same way, as we shall see, the stylistic information provided by dictionaries must not be seen as a fixed truth but rather as a sort of general guideline, which leaves room for the experience of the text. Ideally there is a complementary relationship between the information given in dictionaries and the interpretation of the text.

Suppose we did not know the stylistic meaning of *lousy* (1.3). We would find the following information in dictionaries:

- **a)** *(infested)* verlaust; **be lousy with money** *(coll.)* im Geld schwimmen *(ugs)*; lausig viel Geld haben *(ugs.)*; **places with lousy foreigners** von Ausländern wimmelnde Orte **b)** *(sl.)* *(disgusting)* ekelhaft; widerlich; *(very poor)* lausig *(ugs.)* mies *(ugs.)*; **feel lousy:** sich mies *(ugs.)* od. miserabel fühlen; **men are lousy at housework** Männer stellen sich bei der Hausarbeit miserabel an *(Duden-Oxford)*

- **1.***Slang.* very mean or unpleasant: *a lousy thing to do* **2.***Slang.* inferior or bad: *this is a lousy film.* **3.** infested with lice. **4.** (foll. by *with*) *Slang.* provided with an excessive amount (of): *he's lousy with money.* (CED)

- **1** ...covered with LICE **2** *infml* very bad, unpleasant, useless, etc. **3** ...*infml* **a** filled with **b** having plenty of (esp. money) (DCE)

- **1** If you say that something is **lousy,** you mean that it is of very low quality or that you do not like it at all; an informal use. EG *The food is execrable, the hotels are lousy, the people are rude......***4** A person or animal that is **lousy** has lice on their body or in their hair. *(Collins-COBUILD)*

First of all, stylistic labelling must be seen in connection with polysemy. It is not words but the meanings of a words that are stylistically marked. Thus *lousy* in its meaning "covered with lice" is stylistically unmarked or neutral, whereas in its meaning "bad, inferior, unpleasant" it is marked.

Furthermore, the labels are not identical in the various dictionaries. For the same referential meaning we find a variety of labels: *sl. (slang), ugs. (German: umgangssprachlich), infml (informal).* What do these labels imply stylistically? In the *Duden-Oxford slang* is defined as "especially colloquial and expressive; often used only by particular groups" and *ugs.,* the label used for the German translations, is defined as "everyday conversational language; not generally written, but would not cause offence or ridicule" (p.18). The CED defines *sl.(slang)* in a similar way to the Duden-Oxford: it "refers to words or senses that are informal and restricted in context, for example, to members of a particular social or cultural group. Slang words are inappropriate in formal speech or writing." (p.X). *Infml* in the DCE is defined as "used especially in conversation, in letters between friends, etc." (F46) In Collins-COBUILD we find: "Formality differs between spoken and written English. An expression which is quite normal in conversation might look very informal if it was written down; so *formal* and *informal* are just general guides, and you can use more informal English in speech than in writing." (p. XX).

Which stylistic features, then, are the important ones for our translation? Is it the written-spoken contrast or do we in addition have to retain the group-usage feature?

Shall we make use of what the Duden-Oxford offers? What is to be preferred - *lausig* or *mies?* Or should we use German teenager slang, for instance something like *ätzend,* although such a word would soon become outdated? Or is Heinrich Böll's rather moderate *verflixte Kindheit* the more adequate translation? (cf. J.D. Salinger, *Der Fänger im Roggen,* Nach der ersten Übersetzung

(Zürich 1954) neu durchgesehen und bearbeitet von Heinrich Böll. Reinbek: Rowohlt 1966)

Here again text-linguistic concepts and models will be helpful to understand what goes on in this act of communication. Crystal and Davy, as we saw in the chapter on pragmatic analysis, have offered a "scenic" model of "dimensions of situational constraint" (Crystal/Davy 1969: 64ff.), which has been adopted by House(1977) and Hönig & Kussmaul(1982) for translation purposes, to explain the correlation between non-linguistic situational features and language use. For our text item DISCOURSE features, such as SPEECH vs. WRITING and STATUS features, such as SOCIAL ROLE RELATIONSHIP and SOCIAL ATTITUDE and also SINGULARITY would be relevant explanatory concepts (cf. House 1977: 44ff., Crystal/Davy 1969: 76f.).

An analysis of the text will show us that it has a number of linguistic features typical of speech:

* contractions such as *you'll, don't;* simple syntax, with sentences joined together by *and;*
* words and phrases typical for spoken language, such as *lousy, crap, stuff, pretty personal, touchy, goddam;*
* meta-communicative phrases used for addressing the listener: *if you really want to hear about it..., I don't feel like going into it;*
* vagueness features (cf. Crystal/Davy 1969:114; Crystal/Davy 1975: 111ff.), such as *and all, or anything.*

Some of these features also imply intimate social distance and an equal-to-equal SOCIAL ROLE RELATIONSHIP, e.g. the words *crap, stuff, pretty personal, goddam etc.,* and also the metacommunicative "chatty" phrases like *if you really want to hear about it..., I don't feel like going into it..., I'm not going to tell you...*

The information gained from dictionaries is thus corroborated by stylistic analysis. Dictionary labels such as *informal* for words like *lousy* certainly point in the direction of relevant DISCOURSE and SOCIAL ROLE RELATIONSHIP features of our text, and when translating it one should try to reproduce these features in order to create the desired effects.

What about the *slang* label found in dictionaries? Are there features in our passage that support the idea that it contains group language? By the use of linguistic methods it will be difficult to draw a line between dimensions like social role relationship and discourse on the one hand and what Crystal and Davy call in-group slang (Crystal/Davy 1969:103, 114) on the other. Some of the words, such as *lousy, stuff, goddam* may have been in-group slang words originally, but are now part of the common core of the English vocabulary used in speech among friends.

Just as dictionaries have their limitations because they cannot comprise all the necessary aspects of an act of communication so linguistic analysis has its restrictions too, especially when the text to be translated is a literary one. We will have to turn to literary analysis in order to find out about in-group slang and the narrator's specific use of language. Lundquist (1979) has observed that Holden Caulfield, the hero of the novel and the narrator of our passage, speaks like other teenagers of his time and place and constantly repeats their phrases like *and all* and *I really did* (Lundquist 1979:57). In many places Holden's language seems to be typical schoolboy vulgarity. However, his language is no mere imitation of real-life teenage slang. It is an artefact, used by Salinger to characterize his hero, and as such would fit into Crystal and Davy's SINGU-LARITY dimension (Crystal/Davy 19969:76f.) Holden uses rough language because he wants to appear older than he is and because he wants to fit in with his idea of the adult world (Lundquist 1979:56). Holden's is a carefully constructed language with a narrow choice of often repeated words like *lousy, pretty, crumby, terrific, quite, old* and *stupid* (Lundquist 1979:58).

All these artistic devices should be reflected in translation, and since there is such a limited, repeated number of slang words Holden uses, one should be careful to choose a similar array of target language words in order to create comparable effects.

Böll's *verflixte Kindheit* certainly sounds much too tame in this respect. The equivalents offered by Duden-Oxford, *lausig, mies* seem to be more in line with the results of literary analysis. In the light of Lundquist's interpretation one might even consider *beschissene Kindheit.*

I have dealt with this example at some length in order to show that stylistic information, just as any other information from dictionaries, ought to be supplemented by textual analysis, be it linguistic or literary, in order to find out about the relevant aspects of the meaning of words.

5.6 Teaching the use of dictionaries

For some years now the European Association for Lexicography (EURALEX) at its conferences has had a section called "dictionaries from the user's perspective". The aim of this section is to adjust dictionaries to meet the needs of user-groups such as language learners and translators. It is hoped that in future editions of English dictionaries the results of these discussions will become visible. When looking at the behaviour and attitudes of dictionary users, however, one might sometimes ask oneself if it would not be a good idea to have a EURALEX section on "users from the dictionary makers' point of view" in order to adjust users to the possibilities and limitations of dictionaries.

The average dictionary user has a very naive approach to words and their meanings. The analysis of TAPs discussed in the first Chapter showed that students often misused bilingual dictionaries. It will have become clear, I hope, what we can expect of bilingual dictionaries, what their limitations are, and when we have to use monolingual ones. The use of both bilingual and monolingual dictionaries needs to be learnt.

In a translation training syllabus, there should be a special course on the use of dictionaries or at least some hours should be allotted to this topic within a course. There should be a general survey of what types of dictionaries there are, some information on what they can be used for and how their entries are structured.

In order to be able to extract the maximum of information from definitions and examples in dictionaries, students should have some knowledge of the basic concepts of lexicography, which include structural semantics with notions such as synonymy, hyponymy, polysemy, homonymy, collocation, connotation and distinctive features. Looking up the meanings of words and the equivalents in dictionaries are only part of the truth, however. In many cases we will not find the truth in dictionaries at all. We will then need techniques of analysing meaning in context.

Some strategy tips have evolved from our discussion of the examples. The denotative meaning of words can be gained from the definitions and examples in monolingual dictionaries. With a knowledge of comprehension processes at the back of our minds we are aware that foregrounding and suppression of features may take place, which means that we may have to interpret the relevant feature(s) from the definitions. We then have to test the features which we inferred, against the context. If the features found fit the context, the definition in the dictionary or part of it can be used as a paraphrase for our translation, or to stimulate other translation equivalents.

If the features do not fit the context, we can try to infer different features from the examples provided by the dictionary, and we then test these new features against the context. If they fit, we can use the examples in the dictionary to stimulate a translation.

If we cannot find any useful information in dictionaries, complementary techniques of text analysis can be used in order to infer the relevant semantic features of a given word from its context. There are a number of techniques:

In the case of the meaning of performative verbs, we can infer its relevant features from the meaning of the proposition it introduces. We can also use parts of the context which collocate with the word in question. As a general technique we can use theme and rheme progression.

For finding out about the connotative or stylistic meaning of words there is a similarly twofold technique. We can look for stylistic labels of the words in question in dictionaries. Note: not words but meanings are stylistically marked! If the labels make sense in the context surrounding the word, we can try to find matching translation equivalents.

If we cannot find fitting labels in dictionaries or if the labels are too vague, we can make use of text analysis and apply the model of descriptive stylistics. The situational dimensions which result from our analysis will then have to be mirrored in the translation.

If even the labels for situational dimensions are too vague, we can use literary analysis - for instance, we can look at the typical speech of a character - the results of which we then try to reproduce in our translation.

Chapter 6

Evaluation and errors

6.1 Opposing views among teachers of translation

Opinions on errors often vary considerably. In the first Chapter we tried to find
the reasons why some errors occurred. We analysed them from a psycholinguistic point of view, trying to trace what might have happened in the translator's mind. Let us look again at one of the examples used in the first Chapter and
see what happened when two teachers of translation tried to grade the error in a
students' intermediate test. Here is the passage again:

> On the outback trail in Asia time is distorted. Young travellers, clothed in soiled
> cotton, spend hours waiting, resting on their propped back-packs filled with the
> barest of necessities: toiletries, a change of clothes, a sleeping bag, perhaps a tent,
> almost certainly a diary. Many of them, unused to Eastern food, will fall ill in
> cheap hotels...
> Graduates of many British and American Universities, and from many other parts
> of the world, are postponing entry into their national work-forces to venture
> overseas and experience the world at first hand. A survey of first-year graduates
> by the Career Services Office in Oxford shows that the number planning to travel
> and take temporary work abroad has increased significantly during the last five
> years...
> (*The Illustrated London News*, Spring 1991)

The phrase *experience the world at first hand,* it may be remembered, was
translated by a student by *um zunächst einmal die Welt kennenzulernen.* The
two teachers assessing the translation agreed that a more faithful version would
have been *um die Welt aus eigener Anschauung kennenzulernen,* but they did
not agree on how to grade the error.

Teacher A's verdict was that this was a very serious error. She argued that
at first hand never had the meaning of the adverb *zunächst* ("first of all"). The
notion of physical experience expressed in *at first hand,* she said, was completely lost in the translation. The student in her opinion displayed a serious
deficiency in foreign language competence. A knowledge of basic idioms such as
"at first hand", she argued, was an indispensable requirement for students before
they embarked on a course of professional translation.

Teacher B agreed that *at first hand* does not have the same meaning as "first of all", but he argued that the translation, although incorrect as a literal translation, makes sense within the context and does not distort the meaning of the text. The temporal notion, he said, was indeed supported by the immediately preceding context. As far as the physical experience expressed in the English idiom was concerned, this was rendered in the first lines of the text by the detailed scenic description of students travelling in Asia. One might even say that the phrase "at first hand" was redundant in the text. In the translation there was thus no loss of information. As a consequence, one should not talk of an error here and the candidate should not be penalized.

These are opposing views not uncommon in translation teaching. The first one is the typical *foreign language teacher's view.* It is centred on the word or phrase as an isolated unit and it is also centred on the student as a learner of a foreign language. This type of assessment of errors does not so much take into consideration the communicative function of words and phrases within passages within texts within situations within cultures but centres on the foreign language competence of the student. What happened here is a mixing up of symptom description with diagnosis. The question which teacher A asked was not "Does the error impede communication?" but "What is the reason for the error?" This may be explained by the fact that in error analysis in foreign language teaching looking for the reasons has always been the predominant approach (cf.Corder 1973:256ff.; Brinkmann in Schröder et al.(eds.) 1977:71f.). Thus "basic" errors resulting from the mixing up of simple idioms and lexical items, ignorance of grammatical rules, lack of basic vocabulary etc. are regarded as very serious and are heavily penalized.

The second view is the one proposed in this book. It is *the professional translator's view.* Error assessment is focused on *the communicative function* of the word, phrase or sentence in question. Distortion of meaning must be seen within the text as a whole and with regard to the translation assignment and the receptor of the translation. When adopting the receptor's point of view in the following sections I shall use the psycholinguistic approach discussed in the previous chapters without explicitly repeating my principles in each case. When the opportunity arises, I shall also occasionally, for the sake of contrast, assess the errors from the foreign language teaching point of view in order to show how things should not be done in professional translation courses. It may very well be that what is a mistake from a language teaching point of view is no mistake from a communicative point of view.

Here is another typical example. A student had to translate a text about people trying to make their way through Israel during the Lebanese war:

> They would hit the road from Tiberias to Ber Shean and dodge between the trailers taking tanks and armoured personnel carriers to the Lebanon front. *(The Sunday Times, 10 October 1982)*

The student translated: *Sie...schlängelten sich zwischen Lastwagen (trucks) hindurch*. One of the examiners insisted on a "more precise" translation of *trailers*. The translation the examiner had in mind was *Sattelschlepper*. From a language teaching point of view one might say that the student did not know the difference between *lorry* or *truck* and *trailer*, but does this really matter in the translation? The scene, one might argue, is described just as vividly by using "Lastwagen".

There is an interesting distinction proposed by Pym, who talks of *binary and non-binary errors* (Pym 1992:279ff.) Binary errors are those choices which are clearly wrong. Binarism is the typical approach of foreign language teaching and is concerned with solutions that are either right or wrong, with rules of grammar, "correct" vocabulary, spelling etc. Non-binarism, according to Pym, should be the approach of professional translation teaching. It is concerned with selection from potential target text variants. Typical judgements are "It's correct, but..."

The non-binary approach, I believe, is much more appropriate. It takes account of the fact that evaluation is not only a qualitative but also a quantitative concept. The non-binary approach is basically the same as the *maxim of the sufficient degree of precision* proposed in Chapter 4 (cf. also Hönig and Kussmaul 1982:58ff.). Thus, if in the example just quoted *trailers* had been translated by *Eisenbahnen* (trains), this would be an error that could be assessed by a binary approach. *Eisenbahnen* would clearly be wrong because it does not make any sense at all in this context. The choice between *Lastwagen, Sattelschlepper* or also *Lastwagen mit Anhängern*, however, is a non-binary decision, because it is open to argument how precise one should be in order to create the effect intended by that description.

The notion of non-binary errors and the maxim of the necessary degree of precision in translation are part of a communicative approach to the evaluation of translations. This approach is favoured by an increasing number of specialists in translation studies (e.g. Hönig, House, Kupsch-Losereit, Kussmaul, Nord, Pym, Sager). One of its advantages is that it provides us with more objective standards than the binary language teaching approach. The assessment of errors in language teaching traditionally takes into consideration the stage of proficiency that can be expected of the student, and the "seriousness" of a mistake is regarded from a pedagogical point of view. This means that due account has to be taken of who the student is and what level they are at in their studies. Subjective considerations are inevitably involved here.

When using the communicative approach we do not have to think about the person who produced the translation. In order to evaluate a translation we do not have to know what went on in the student's mind when producing an error. We can restrict ourselves to the effect the error has on the target reader.

In psycholinguistic terms, we are trying to imagine what kind of *scene* is created in the target reader by a particular linguistic *frame* used by the translator (cf. Chapter 1). One might argue, however, that this approach is just as speculative since we do not really know what goes on in a reader's mind, and that our speculations instead of being retrospective are prospective, but are speculations nevertheless. Still, I believe, it is easier to imagine oneself as an average reader than as an unsuccessful student translator.

The fact that we do not consider the translators as learners when evaluating their translations does not mean that we never ask why they produced errors. As I have shown in the first Chapter, the reasons for students' errors, i.e. unsuccessful solution processes, should form the empirical basis for translation teaching, and one way of finding out about the reasons is protocols of the translation process. It should be clear, however, that evaluation, that is, description of the symptoms, and looking for the reasons of errors, i.e. diagnosis, are two distinct categories (cf. section 1.1). Here we are dealing with the description of the symptoms, and this can best be done by observing how the patient interacts with other people.

6.2 Categories for evaluation

In the analysis of texts and their translations pragmatic categories such as cultural, situational and text-typological adequacy refer to relatively large linguistic units whereas categories such as meanings of words, grammatical forms and orthography are normally focused on smaller units. As a result, one might draw the conclusion that pragmatic errors ought to get more negative marks than, say, word errors. Thus pragmatic errors would, for instance, count two points and word errors would count one point. However, if we agree that evaluation is a quantitative, non-binary concept along the lines suggested by Pym and along the maxim of the sufficient degree of precision suggested in this book, there is no simple and convenient way of grading. In each individual case we will have to ask ourselves: How far-reaching is the error? Does it distort the sense of a sentence, of a passage or even of the whole text? Does it inhibit or even destroy communication? Does it weaken the psychological effect? It may very well be that what looks as a simple orthographic error does in fact change the meaning of a whole sentence, and what looks as a simple error in word meaning distorts the meaning of the entire text.

6.2.1 *Cultural adequacy*

In Enid Blyton's book *Five go to Smuggler's Top*, there are some passages which have produced quite a few problems for the German translator and which can serve to illustrate how to evaluate a translation and grade errors.

Uncle Quentin has an idea

Next morning the wind was still high, but the fury of the gale was gone. The fishermen on the beach were relieved to find that their boats had suffered very little damage. But word soon went round about the accident to Kirrin Cottage, and a few sightseers came up to marvel at the sight of the great, uprooted tree, lying heavily on the little house.

The children rather enjoyed the importance of relating how nearly they had escaped with their lives. In the light of the day it was surprising what damage the big tree had done. It had cracked the roof of the house like an eggshell, and the rooms upstairs were in a terrible mess.

The woman who came up from the village to help Aunt Fanny during the day exclaimed at the sight: "Why, Mam, it'll take weeks to set that right!" she said. "Have you got on to the builders, Mam? I'd get them up here right away and let them see what's to be done."

"I'm seeing to things, Mrs. Daly", said Uncle Quentin. "my wife has had a great shock. She is not fit to see to things herself. The first thing to do is to decide what is to happen to the children. They can't remain here while there are no usable bedrooms."

(Enid Blyton, *Five go to Smuggler's Top,* Leicester:Knight's Books 1969, 22)

Onkel Quentin hat einen Einfall

Am nächsten Morgen hatte der Sturm endlich nachgelassen. Es wehte aber noch ein starker Wind. Die Fischer waren erfreut, als sie ihre Boote am Strand nur wenig beschädigt vorfanden.

Das Unglück vom Felsenhaus sprach sich sehr schnell herum. Einige Neugierige machten sich auf, um den großem entwurzelten Baum anzustaunen, der auf das Dach des kleinen Wohnhauses gestürzt war.

Die Kinder kamen sich sehr wichtig vor und berichteten ausführlich wie sie mit knapper Not dem Tode entronnen waren. Jetzt, am hellen Tag, zeigte sich erst richtig, welch großen Schaden der mächtige Baum angerichtet hatte. Wie eine Eierschale hatte er das Dach durchbrochen. Die oberen Räume waren in einem verheerenden Zustand.

Die Frau, die vom Dorf heraufkam und tagsüber Tante Fanny bei der Arbeit half, sagte sofort beim Anblick der Zerstörung: "Da werden Wochen draufgehen, bis das in Ordnung ist. Haben Sie schon die Maurer bestellt?"

"Das mache ich selber, Frau Dahle", antwortete Onkel Quentin an Tante Fanny's Stelle. Meine Frau fühlt sich nicht wohl, sie kann sich nicht darum kümmern. Das wichtigste ist, daß wir beraten, was mit den Kindern geschieht. Sie können nicht hierbleiben, ihre Schlafräume sind unbenutzbar."

(Enid Blyton, *5 Freunde auf Schmugglerjagd,* (Deutsche Bearbeitung von Dr. Werner Lincke), München: Bertelsmann,n.d., 23f.)

Enid Blyton's story is embedded in the British culture. There is the name of the house *Kirrin Cottage,* and there are the names of the people, and there is something specifically British in the way the people talk. There seems to be a tradition today in the translation of literature, as Reiss and Vermeer (1984:90ff.) have pointed out, of not transferring the plot into the target culture. As readers we enjoy reading about (and watching on TV) the fates of our heroes in foreign, often "exotic" cultures. It adds to the excitement of living within these fictitious worlds.

Werner Lincke does not seem to follow this tradition. He calls his translation a *Bearbeitung* (adaptation) perhaps implying by this term a greater freedom in cultural transfer. Thus, he changes *Kirrin Cottage* to *Felsenhaus* (cliff-house), although this does not represent a typical naming convention in Germany (German houses are identified by streets and numbers.). However, by this translation he is perhaps trying to suggest that this is a name given to the house by the children. Aunt Fanny's help is called *Frau Dahle* which sounds sufficiently German, and so does *Tante Fanny* (a shortened form of Franziska) although in this case the English name has not been translated. Within this German sounding group of names, leaving the uncle's name (*Quentin*) untranslated makes it, one might feel, sound foreign or strangely archaic to German ears.

The translation, one might say, is not quite satisfactory here. As far as cultural embedding is concerned, it lacks coherence, one of the basic requirements of a translation, and indeed a text (cf. Halliday/Hasan 1976:23, Reiss/Vermeer 1984:115ff., Hatim/Mason 1990:194ff., Baker 1992:218ff.). Lincke, it might be argued, should have used either English or German names throughout and should not have mixed them.

Now, I proposed that each instant of criticism and each error in a translation should be graded according to its communicative effect. In true pragmatic and indeed psycholinguistic manner we shall then relate the text to its receptor, i.e. its readers. Enid Blyton's book is a children's book, and the question is whether children really are disturbed by this seeming lack of coherence. In fact, I tested the German translation in this respect with my fifteen year old son, and he felt that *Quentin* was as good as any German Christian name. He thought, that *Quentin* was a normal name he had not heard before. I am aware of the fact that this single "case-history" is not a sufficiently large empirical basis to draw valid conclusions.   Still, an explanation might be that children, because their vocabulary is in the process of being constantly enlarged, will not only come across new names but indeed new words all the time, and they will accept words much more easily than adults. Children are not linguistic purists. The situation is different with adults. I also gave my adult students the translation to read, and they told me that *Quentin* was a strange name. Thus this instance of lack of coherence may be a defect for adult readers, but most likely not for children.

From a communicative point of view this lack of coherence is not to be graded as a mistake.

One might still ask, however, whether the translator should not have used English names for places and people in order to create that foreign atmosphere which is so conducive to flights of imagination, especially since this seems to be a general tradition in translating. Should he not have conformed to that norm and used *Kirrin Cottage* and *Mrs. Daly* and other English names wherever possible. As far as the effect of the story is concerned, placing it in a foreign country will increase its fascination also for children. There are classic children's tales that take place in "exotic" surroundings, e.g. *Robinson Crusoe, Gulliver's Travels, Swiss Family Robinson, Treasure Island,* to name but a few. Thus, not using English names whenever possible, from this type of pragmatic viewpoint ought to be criticized as a quite serious omission and defect.

We have discussed conventions of cultural embedding in literary translation. For non-fiction texts such as textbooks, user manuals, scholarly articles etc. the situation is different. For these types of texts the creation of a foreign atmosphere and the illusion of a fictitious world are not normally part of their purpose. Adaptations to the target culture may therefore be functionally adequate.

A typical case are the following sentences in the first Chapter of David Crystal's *Linguistics*:

> Most people who have read an introduction to linguistics over the past fifteen years or so ... have had a vested interest in getting into the subject. They were students of English or modern languages, teachers of various languages (particularly of English to foreigners), translators, academics in related disciplines (such as sociology or psychology), and other 'professionals'.
> (David Crystal, *Linguistics*. Harmondsworth: Penguin Books 1971:9)

In the German translation the passage reads:

> Die meisten Leser von Einführungen in die Linguistik während der letzten fünfzehn Jahre ... hatten ein berufsbezogenes Interesse daran, sich in dieses Fachgebiet einzuarbeiten. Es handelte sich um Studenten der neuphilologischen Fächer, um Lehrer verschiedener Sprachen, Übersetzer, Akademiker in verwandten Disziplinen (z.B. der Soziologie oder Psychologie) und andere "Profis".
> (David Crystal, *Einführung in die Linguistik*. Aus dem Englischen übersetzt und für den deutschen Leser bearbeitet von Cristoph Gutknecht, Axel Horstmann und Yngve Olsson. Stuttgart: Kohlhammer 1975:7)

When talking about people interested in linguistics, Crystal refers to the situation in Britain and America. The translators adapted the text (as they say in the subtitle) to the German situation and replaced *students of English or modern languages* by *Studenten der neuphilologischen Fächer* and *teachers ..par-*

ticularly of English to foreigners by *Lehrer verschiedener Sprachen.* The translators' decision to adapt the text was certainly the right thing to do. If they had talked of *Englischstudenten* or *Studenten anderer Fremdsprachen* the German reader would have asked: what about the Germanisten (professors of German)? It was not least the Germanisten who in the late sixties and early seventies made modern linguistics a subject at German universities. If they had talked of *Englischlehrer für Ausländer* the German reader would have been really at a loss, because this type of teacher, naturally, does not exist in Germany.

Obviously, the adaptation makes sense to the German reader. Critics conceding cultural adaptation but still pedantically sticking to cultural equivalence on the word level might argue that the phrase *teachers ..particularly of English to foreigners* should have been translated by *besonders Deutschlehrer für Ausländer.* Surely, this would mean narrowing down the group of people for no obvious reason. In fact, in Germany linguistics started playing an important role in foreign language teaching in general in the seventies, and it was not before several years had passed that university courses for teachers of German to foreigners were established (probably the best known one being in Munich).

Who is to decide whether cultural adaptation should take place or not? If they use a communicative approach to their work, translators should be able to decide for themselves. They will be well advised, however, to consult their clients in this matter. In translation classes, when my students come up with solutions like the ones quoted I do not hesitate to give them additional good points. As Nord rightly said, we should do everything we can to motivate our students, and a positive evaluation of problems solved will certainly help in this respect (cf. Nord 1988: 203). In tests, I give my students an oriented translation task, in other words, I tell them the purpose of their translation, who their prospective readership is, and sometimes, in order to get them on the right path, I also tell them if they should adapt the text to the target culture or leave it within the source culture. Once these decisions have been made for them, there still remains the task of actually recognizing the words or phrases that have to be adapted and of finding a sensible adaptation.

6.2.2 *Situational adequacy*

In the text by Enid Blyton quoted above there is a dialogue which may serve to illustrate the notion of situational adequacy. For convenience sake I shall repeat it:

> The woman who came up from the village to help Aunt Fanny during the day exclaimed at the sight: "Why, Mam, it'll take weeks to set that right!" she said. "Have you got on to the builders, Mam? I'd get them up here right away and let them see what's to be done."

"I'm seeing to things, Mrs. Daly", said Uncle Quentin. "my wife has had a great shock. She is not fit to see to things herself. The first thing to do is to decide what is to happen to the children. They can't remain here while there are no usable bedrooms."

Mrs. Daly's utterances are marked by a number of situational dimensions (cf. Chapter 3.1). First of all, they are marked by MEDIUM. By the use of contractions (*it'll, I'd, what's*) and phrasal verbs (*got on, get them up*) and by the use of interjections, such as *why*, they are typical of the spoken medium. Moreover, Mrs. Daly's utterances are marked by the dimension of SOCIAL ROLE RELATIONSHIP, apparent in the form of address (*Mam*) which implies a lower-to-higher relationship.

Uncle Quentin's words are also marked as speech by contractions such as *I'm, can't*. The actual choice of words, however, reveals a certain precision, which can be interpreted as a sign of SOCIAL ATTITUDE, that is, a certain distance between himself and Mrs. Daly. Thus he uses the rather formal *she is not fit* and not simply *can't, decide* and not *think about, remain* and not *stay*. One and the same linguistic feature may sometimes be interpreted as a sign of more than one situational dimension. Uncle Quentin's rather precise way of talking could also be seen as typical middle class speech, and would thus reflect SOCIAL CLASS.

The stylistic features of the dialogue add to the vividness of that little scene. If this scenic vividness is to be retained in the translation, the characters' speech will have to display a similar stylistic complexity and variety. Does it?

Die Frau, die vom Dorf heraufkam und tagsüber Tante Fanny bei der Arbeit half, sagte sofort beim Anblick der Zerstörung: "Da werden Wochen draufgehen, bis das in Ordnung ist. Haben Sie schon die Maurer bestellt?"

"Das mache ich selber, Frau Dahle", antwortete Onkel Quentin an Tante Fannys Stelle. "Meine Frau fühlt sich nicht wohl, sie kann sich nicht darum kümmern. Das wichtigste ist, daß wir beraten, was mit den Kindern geschieht. Sie können nicht hierbleiben, ihre Schlafräume sind unbenutzbar."

Lincke in his translation has to some extent made use of the MEDIUM features of spoken language in Mrs. Daly's speech (e.g. *da werden* and not *es werden*), but he has not exploited all the possibilities available. There is no interjection in her speech in German, and strangely her last sentence remains untranslated although this would have allowed him to use additional stylistically marked forms. Also, the failure to translate this sentence has resulted in some distortion of the sense of the dialogue. When Mrs. Daly asks Uncle Quentin *Haben Sie schon die Maurer bestellt?* and he answers *Das mache ich selber, Frau Dahle* (I'll do it myself) the reader thinks that Uncle Quentin will repair the house himself. This is an error, however, which would have to be discussed under the category of meaning. For a translation which adds more MEDIUM features and which also preserves the sense of Uncle Quentin's utterance I would suggest:

"Ach Gott, Mam, das wird ja Wochen dauern, bis das wieder in Ordnung ist. Haben Sie schon die Handwerker bestellt? Mir müßen die gleich herkommen und sehen, was man machen kann."
"Darum kümmere ich mich, Mrs. Daly," antwortete Onkel Quentin...

The rendering of the SOCIAL CLASS features of Uncle Quentins speech in the translation is a problem because there are no class dialects in German. The SOCIAL ROLE RELATIONSHIP expressed additionally in *Mam* could in former times have been rendered by *Gnädige Frau*, but this is rather dated now, except in Austria. Earlier, it will be remembered, we criticized the translator for not having left the story within the context of British culture. If he had done so, he could have used the English form of address here, which is, in fact, a typical translators' convention. In novels, soap operas, plays etc. we always get *Sir, Madam, Miss, Mrs*. However, it is doubtful whether the SOCIAL ROLE RELATIONSHIP implications would have been noticed by German readers. One would perhaps have to consider whether the lower-to-higher relationship can be expressed by different linguistic means, for instance by forms of politeness in other places of the text.

The translation of Uncle Quentin's speech preserves the situational features quite well. By inserting "an Tante Fannys Stelle" the translator makes the role of the speaker more explicit. Syntactically, Uncle Quentin's words sound as if they were spoken, and at the same time they retain a certain degree of formality (*beraten* and not *mal überlegen, unbenutzbar* and not *kann man nicht mehr benutzen*). There are, however, semantic errors in the translation of his speech, which I shall deal with below.

It will have become clear, I hope, that when evaluating the translation we do not use language teaching arguments such as: by leaving out a sentence the translator has shown that he does not know how to translate so-and-so many English words. When evaluating the translation from a communicative point of view we may say that as far as situational adequacy is concerned it is not completely inappropriate but it could still be improved. We do get some kind of "scenic" effect, but not as vividly as in the English text. I certainly would not give additional good points for brilliant solutions here.

In Chapter 3 on pragmatic analysis we saw that there is a close connection between situation and text type. The situational dimensions PROVINCE and MODALITY, above all, seem to be constitutive for text typological conventions. As far as PROVINCE is concerned, when assessing the quality of translations the correct use of the technical vocabulary of a professional activity will no doubt play an important role. In texts written for experts, technical vocabulary will not only promote quick and easy comprehension but its mastery will also add to the prestige of the author of the text. Apart from vocabulary there are the more subtle conventions related to MODALITY. For example, in British scholarly articles directive speech acts are often performed by the use of the imperative. Thus we have sentences like *Consider the following example.* In German texts of this type we typically have *Betrachten wir das folgende Beispiel.* But for summaries on book covers, which apart from being informative have a certain advertising function, there are different conventions. In a translation test, I had my students translate the text on the back flap of a book on handwriting analysis, part of which ran

> Learn how to make it (graphonomy) work for you, and you will enter a new world of understanding and sensibility.

This was translated by a student as

> Lernen wir, sie zu unserem Nutzen einzusetzen, und wir werden ein neues Verständnis und Einfühlungsvermögen erlangen.

Using the pronoun of the first person plural would have been correct when addressing the reader in a scholarly article, but in summaries on book covers the communicative point is completely missed by using this convention. The translation should have run

> Lernen Sie, die Graphonomie zu Ihrem Nutzen einzusetzen, und Sie werden ein neues Verständnis und Einfühlungsvermögen erlangen.

Obviously, mistakes of this kind cannot be treated lightly because the misuse of conventions distorts the intention of the text.

6.2.3 *Speech acts*

In Enid Blyton's text, Mrs. Daly performs a number of speech acts which are not adequately rendered in the translation. To begin with, by exclaiming *Why, Mam...* Mrs. Daly shows surprise at what she perceives, and according to Searle she performs an illocutionary act of the *expressive* type (Searle 1976:12). This speech act is completely left out in the translation. The translator also left out her utterance *I'd get them up here right away and let them see what's to be done.* We saw that this omission distorts the sense of the dialogue between her and Uncle Quentin. More specifically, by saying what she would do in this situation Mrs. Daly is making a *suggestion* or giving *advice*, a *directive* speech act in Searle's typology (1976:11). Finally, when Uncle Quentin says *I'm seeing to things, Mrs. Daly* he *replies* to this advice and *points out* that he is the person that should be addressed thus, according to Searle (1976:10f.), performing two simultaneous *representative* speech acts. Moreover, his speech act could be interpreted as *putting Mrs.Daly in her place*, one of Searle's *directives*. Uncle Quentin would thus want to show that Mrs. Daly is not in a position to give advice. As we saw earlier (Chapter 3) in the text-specimen taken from A.S.Neill's autobiography, there is often no single performative verb to describe the illocution of an utterance, because in actual life when making an utterance we often do several things at the same time. We are faced with a similar situation here again.

These complexities are not preserved in the translation. Are they important? If we take the text to be a literary one, the characters by their way of talking expose part of their personality and show their attitude toward each other. As readers we may experience Mrs. Daly as an emotional, spontaneous, energetic woman who perhaps talks a little too much. Uncle Quentin seems to be a practical kind of person who keeps up social distinctions. This impression would, of course, have to be confirmed by observing how the characters behave throughout the book. I think, however, one would be justified in saying that the translation's inadequacy on the illocutionary level is a serious defect.

Looking at illocutions is a useful procedure when analysing dialogues. It is useful also when analysing communication between the writer of a text and its reader. For instance, *Instructions* in English leaflets are typically performed by using the imperative, e.g.:

PRECAUTIONS
* Operate the set only on 3 V dc.
* For ac operation, use the ac power adapter recommended for this set.
* For car battery operation, use the car battery cord recommended for this set.
(Sony Stereo Cassette-player WM-22)

The German translation sold with the cassette player reads:

ZUR BESONDEREN BEACHTUNG
* Betreiben Sie das Gerät nur an 3 V Gleichspannung.
* Zum Betrieb mit Netzstrom verwenden Sie den für dieses Gerät empfohlenen Netzadapter.
* Zum Anschluß an die Autobatterie verwenden Sie nur das für dieses Gerät empfohlene Autobatteriekabel.

Instructions belong to Searle's class of *directives* and are used to make the hearer or reader perform some future action (Searle 1976, 11). In English leaflets, manuals and operating instructions this speech act is typically indicated by the imperative. In other text types or situations, different illocutionary force indicators are used. In polite conversations, for instance, we often use indirect speech acts such as: "Would you pass me the salt?" In German leaflets, manuals, etc. the conventional form most often used is the infinitive, but as we saw earlier there are also other forms, such as the imperative or the use of *müssen*, depending on specific contexts within these text types.

In the German translation of the Walkman leaflet the form used to indicate the speech act is ambiguous. *Verwenden Sie* can either be the imperative or the polite form of the second person singular indicative, depending on word order. In the sentences quoted, after the adverbial phrase there is inversion, and seen from a grammatical point of view we here have an affirmative clause. In order to preserve the imperative clause the word order should have been changed, and the German sentences should have read

- Verwenden Sie zum Betrieb mit Netzstrom den für dieses Gerät empfohlenen Netzadapter.
- Verwenden Sie zum Anschluß an die Autobatterie...

These would have been unambiguous instructions. When trying to evaluate this translation one might argue that the illocution has been changed from instruction to statement, and as a result the reader of the text will not be able to perform the action required of him. We should not make the mistake of seeing the speech act in isolation, however. Our procedure should always be to contextualize the item in question, that is to say, to see the effect it has on the reader taking into account what he knows from context and situation. In the present case the reader has just been given an unambiguous instruction (*Betreiben Sie das Gerät nur an 3 V Gleichspannung*), and he will expect that the instructions will be continued. There is little real danger that he will not know what to do and damage the walkman by misuse. Still, smooth and easy understanding is impeded here. It might very well be that the readers would have to look twice at this sentence before they know what they are supposed to do. I would thus grade the error not as a serious mistake but still as a slight defect of translation.

There is a word-class typically used as illocutionary force indicators and notorious for mistranslations. This word-class has always posed a problem for linguists, because the words it contains have no referential meaning and modify not only words but also the propositional content of sentences, a quality which was, in fact, recognized before the days of speech act theory (cf. Greenbaum 1969, passim). They are sentence adverbials such as *in fact, indeed, actually, anyway, then, now, naturally,* etc.(cf. Kussmaul 1978b, passim). In the text by David Crystal quoted there is a typical example which was also typically mistranslated, and the ironical thing about it is that the translators were themselves linguists. As the illocution of sentences has often to be interpreted within a larger context a more extensive quotation is given:

Why Study Language
Introductory books and courses on linguistics invariably try to get away from their rather complex-sounding titles as soon as they can, by producing a thumb-

nail definition which (it is hoped) will provide a more familiar starting point. This is usually something like 'Linguistics is the scientific study of language'. The authors then proceed to explain exactly why it is important to emphasize that linguistics is language studied *scientifically*, and follow this up by analysing the object of study, language, in some detail. All of which assumes a considerable amount of prior interest and commitment on the part of the reader. It is, after all, no small task to embark on a thorough introduction to linguistics; most books of this kind have four hundred pages or more!
(David Crystal, *Linguistics*. Harmondsworth: Penguin Books 1971:9)

The translators' error occurred when translating the last sentence which contains the adverbial *after all*. In order to give an idea of the lack of textual cohesion (for the term see Halliday/Hasan 1976:23) I shall quote the preceding and succeeding sentences:

Nach dieser Definition versucht man gewöhnlich genauer zu erklären, warum es wichtig ist, das Wort *wissenschaftlich* zu betonen, und geht dann dazu über, den Untersuchungsgegenstand, die Sprache, im einzelnen zu analysieren. All dies setzt ein großes, schon bestehendes Interesse auf seiten des Lesers voraus. Und doch ist es kein leichtes Unterfangen, eine gründliche Einführung in die Linguistik zu schreiben: Die meisten vergleichbaren Bücher umfassen vierhundert Seiten oder sogar mehr. Und es wäre naiv zu erwarten, daß jemand bereit wäre, so viele mit Text, Fußnoten und (recht oft auch) Übungen gefüllte Seiten durch- zuarbeiten, ohne daß er Vorkenntnisse oder ein besonderes Interese an diesen Fragen besäße.
(David Crystal, *Einführung in die Linguistik*. Aus dem Englischen übersetzt und für den deutschen Leser bearbeitet von Cristoph Gutknecht, Axel Horstmann und Yngve Olsson. Stuttgart: Kohlhammer 1975:7)

The sentence adverbial *after all* in the source text expresses an illocution, which is neatly defined by the DCE as *it must be remembered that*. The illocution contained in this definition could be made explicit by the use of a performative verb and paraphrased as: *I ask/request you to remember that,* which again is one of Searle's *directives*. Thus, in order to get an idea of the illocutionary meaning of the sentence adverbial we can either replace it by the definition in the DCE, which will give us

It is, it must be remembered, no small task to embark on a thorough introduction to linguistics

or we can replace it by the performative formula, which will give us

It is, I ask/request you to remember, no small task to embark on a thorough introduction to linguistics

both of which are synonymous sentences. In the German translation the sentence reads:

Und doch ist es kein leichtes Unterfangen, eine gründliche Einführung in die Linguistik zu schreiben.

Und doch could be paraphrased by *in spite of this* (cf. *DCE*) and back-translated as *however,* so that we would get

> It is, however, no small task to embark on a thorough introduction to linguistics.

Obviously, this latter sentence has a different illocution, although one may find it difficult to describe by means of a performative verb. In addition, *embark* is translated as *schreiben,* which would back-translate as *write,* but this shall not be discussed for the moment. A foreign language teacher would perhaps mark the translation of *after all* by *und doch* as a simple mistake of word meaning. Seen from a communicative point of view, however, the translation *und doch* completely distorts the line of thought of the passage.

It can be described by looking at the relationship of the propositional contents of the sentences in question (cf. Kussmaul 1978b:163). In the immediately preceding sentence a prior interest and commitment is attributed to the reader. The sentence introduced by *after all* attributes the quality *no small task* to the reader's action. The relationship between the sentences can be paraphrased by *because.* The reader needs some prior interest etc. *because* reading an introduction to linguistics is no small task. The sentence introduced by *after all* thus gives the reason for the preceding sentence, and a *request to remember* the proposition of the sentence is logically in line with it. An adequate translation which preserves the illocution of the sentence would have been:

> Es ist schließlich kein leichtes Unterfangen, eine gründliche Einführung in die Linguistik zu lesen.

The line of thought of the German translation is completely illogical, if not absurd. It can be paraphrased in the following way: the reader has is a prior interest in linguistics, but, in spite of this interest, writing a book on linguistics is no small task. At this the reader will ask what the connection is between the difficulty of writing a book and the reader's prior interest. The topic of the preceding and following sentences is not writing but reading a book on linguistics. The mistranslation thus seriously disturbs textual cohesion and should therefore be viewed as a serious error.

6.2.4 *Meaning of words*

The translation of *embark* by *schreiben* in the sentence just quoted is a typical error of word meaning resulting most likely from a misinterpretation of the text. *Embark* as a metaphor is potentially ambiguous, but its ambiguity can easily be reduced by looking at the topic of these lines. However, we are not concerned here with the causes of errors, we are concerned with their grading. The error in word meaning in combination with the distortion of the illocution of the sentence, as we saw, seriously impedes communication. Even if the illocution had been preserved, however, *schreiben* would still distort the line of thought. It is important to see that the error does not only change the meaning of the sentence in which it occurs but has even more far-reaching effects. It makes the author's argument look completely nonsensical and thereby disqualifies the author of the book in the eyes of the readers of the translation. David Crystal scarcely deserves this.

There is a similarly far-reaching error in the translation of the title of the first Chapter of David Crystal's book. The title *Why study language* was rendered by the translator-team of linguists as *Sinn und Zweck des Sprachstudiums,* which translates back as *Why study languages?* Linguists above all, one would think, should have been aware that the topic of the book was not foreign language learning but linguistics. They were in fact aware of this, and in the first lines of the chapter translated *linguistics* correctly by *Linguistik.* One might be inclined to excuse this error as a mere slip of attention, and language teachers would probably argue that the normal German equivalent for *language* is indeed *Sprache,* and that the translators have at least shown they know English, and therefore this should not really be counted as a serious mistake.

But what is the communicative effect of the title *Sinn und Zweck des Sprachstudiums?* How does it affect textual cohesion? Titles are used, among other things, to give an idea of what a text is about. They are prominent utterances, because they refer to very large textual units. By looking at the titles of chapters, maybe when leafing through the table of contents of a book in a bookshop, we may try to find out if the information it contains will be useful for us and, hence, if it is worth buying the book. The readers of the translation will be completely misled as to the topic of this chapter. In Fillmore's (1976, 1977) terms, the wrong scenes will be activated in their minds. They will think that the chapter is about studying foreign languages such as French, Italian or English in language schools or in an undergraduate university course. When trying to reconcile their understanding of the title of the chapter with their understanding of the title of the book (*Einführung in die Linguistik*) they may think that the book is about the applied linguistics of foreign language teaching while it is, in fact, an introduction into general linguistics. Thus the error, although it might have been a mere slip, here again has far-reaching communicative effects and should not be dismissed lightly.

We should always consider the consequences and extent of these effects when assessing the seriousness of errors in word meaning. In the passage quoted from Enid Blyton's book the second sentence *But word soon went round about the accident to Kirrin Cottage* was translated as *Das Unglück vom Felsenhaus sprach sich sehr schnell herum.* Language teachers would probably accept this translation without any criticism. *Unglück,* they might feel, is a good equivalent for *accident*. It is offered as a translation by most bilingual dictionaries. If we take on the role of the reader of the translation who does not know the original, however, we will realize that *Unglück* leads to false expectations. The German word *Unglück* implies that people have been killed or at least badly injured, but in the course of the story it becomes clear that everyone is well. There is, and this may have been the reason for the mistranslation, no single word in German that could serve as an equivalent for *accident* in this context, but the meaning can be expressed by the use of a grammatical shift: *Es sprach sich sehr bald herum was mit Kirrin Cottage passiert war* (...what had happened to Kirrin Cottage).

Evaluation in professional translation, it will be remembered, is a quantitative process. Errors in professional translation are typically non-binary, and have to be graded along a scale. The more far-reaching their negative effect is the more serious they are. If we compare the case of *embark - schreiben* and of *Study Language - Sprachstudium* with *accident - Unglück* it will become clear that the semantic disturbances caused by *Unglück* are not as far-reaching as those caused by the other mistakes. Nevertheless, *Unglück* is a defect in semantic textual cohesion.

Gradually moving from serious to less serious semantic mistakes let us look at a line in Enid Blyton's story again. The last line of Uncle Quentin's speech *They* (the children) *can't remain here while there are no usable bedrooms* is translated by Werner Lincke as *Sie können nicht hierbleiben, ihre Schlafräume sind unbenutzbar*. We saw that Uncle Quentin's way of speaking is marked by SOCIAL ATTITUDE and SOCIAL CLASS, and the translator probably tried to take account of this by not choosing the usual word *Schlafzimmer* but *Schlafräume*. The distinction between the two words is, however, not a stylistic, but a semantic one; more precisely, one of referential meaning. *Schlafräume* is used for bedrooms in buildings such as youth hostels and boarding schools and denotes rooms with many beds. Is it a serious mistake in word meaning? I do not think understanding is really impeded here. The reader of the translation has been told a few moments ago: *Die oberen Räume waren in einem verheerenden Zustand,* and he will most likely associate those rooms with the children's' bedrooms he is being told about now. What the reader may feel is that Uncle Quentin uses some German words in a rather unusual way, and may wonder whether his linguistic behaviour is in line with the rest of his character.

6.2.5 *"Language errors"*

This type of error is usually the most important one in foreign language teaching. It includes errors such as wrong use of tenses, prepositions, word order, idioms, collocations etc., and the more "basic" these errors are, the more heavily they are usually penalized. Errors of this type also appear in translations, but our standards for evaluation are, as will have become clear by now, different from the ones used in language teaching. In order to be consistent with our communicative approach, we must try to imagine the effect the misuse of tenses, word order, prepositions etc. has on the target reader. For example, do these mistakes impede comprehension? Do they bring discredit on the author of the text? In the story by Enid Blyton the sentences

> In the light of the day it was surprising what damage the big tree had done. It had cracked the roof of the house like an eggshell

were translated as follows:

> Jetzt, am hellen Tag, zeigte sich erst richtig, welch großen Schaden der mächtige Baum angerichtet hatte. Wie eine Eierschale hatte er das Dach durchbrochen.

First of all, *Eierschale* does not collocate with *durchbrechen*. *Durchbrechen* implies that the object is made of stronger material that an eggshell. A better collocation would be *eingedrückt*. Also, the word order is rather strange. *Wie eine Eierschale* will be understood to refer to *er* (the tree). To obtain the correct reference the word order ought to be *Er hatte das Dach wie eine Eierschale durchbrochen*.

For the target reader I do not think that comprehension is made impossible here, but I would imagine that the wrong word order impedes smooth reading, and readers who are sensitive to collocations and idiomatic phrasing will perhaps feel that the author of the story is not very competent linguistically. Since the original text, as we saw, has literary qualities, this effect would diminish its overall value.

There are cases where "language errors" make it difficult for the reader to grasp the meaning of a text. Here is an example from the instructions leaflet of a Rowenta thermos flask. The stylistic idea of the source text is to personify the flask and have it talk to the user. The last lines run:

> Bei etwas Rücksichtnahme bin ich für Sie lange Zeit ein zuverlässiger Partner. Aber auch ich kann das Opfer eines Materialfehlers oder einer Krankheit werden. In diesem Falle schicken Sie mich bitte an das nächste Rowenta-Service-Center.
> Auf gute Zusammenarbeit
> Ihre Rowenta-Warmhaltekanne

The translation reads:

> With a little consideration I will be a reliable help to you for a long time. However possibly I could have a flaw in my material or some other weakness. In which case please send me to your nearest Rowenta Service Dealer.

Here's to a good working relationship,
Your
Rowenta thermal jug.

The translator manifestly had problems with the English syntax and with the prepositions and conjunctions to the extent that the readers may be puzzled as to what the text really means, i.e. how they are supposed to treat the flask. Moreover, the personification originally intended to add a humorous note to the text is diminished. *Partner* becomes *help* and *Krankheit* becomes *weakness*. Further, the reader will be surprised when reading the penultimate lines, which would rather suggest that a toast is about to be drunk. One begins to wonder what sort of liquid is inside the flask. And finally, the ending of the letter is inappropriate. English letters always use the form *yours* (e.g. *yours sincerely*) in the concluding formula, and not *your*. A more convincing translation might be:

Yours ever,
Your Rowenta thermos flask.

In foreign language teaching, spelling errors are perhaps not marked as seriously as grammatical or lexical ones. In translation, when considering the communicative effect, things can be different. In a translation test, students had to translate the title and first passage of a book on handwriting. The title ran

The Hidden Language of your Handwriting.

It was translated in one case as

Die verborgene Sprache ihrer Handschrift.

I have no objection to the phrasing of the sentence, but not writing *ihrer* with a capital letter changes its meaning. A back-translation would give us *The hidden language of their handwriting* or *The hidden language of her handwriting*. I asked my students what they would expect of a book with this title, and one of them said it reminded her of titles of novels and another was reminded of titles of detective stories. Obviously, this is not merely an orthographic mistake but an error in sentence meaning if not text meaning and cannot be treated lightly.

6.3 Source text defects

In my teaching I am often asked by students what they should do when they are faced with obvious defects in the texts to be translated. The common opinion among lay people and beginner students is that the translator should not be made responsible for these things, and that he or she should follow the maxim "garbage in, garbage out".

This may do for translation as practised in foreign language teaching, but it is not good enough for professional translation. If we want to produce a well functioning text for the target reader we must aim at faultless texts. Let us consider the reaction of the target readers for a moment. Suppose they read a translation which faithfully copies the defects of the original - inappropriate use of vocabulary, misleading sentence structure, illogical argument - then the target readers will come to the conclusion that they are faced with a bad translation. If they are not aware that it is a translation, they will get the impression that they are faced with a badly written original text. The effect, in both cases, is undesirable. Either the author of the text or its translator will appear to be linguistically incompetent. Obviously, no author will want to create this effect, and would want defects corrected.

Things are not quite so easy, however. Translators who tell their clients that the source text is not good enough will often meet with some hostility. There may be several reasons. Linguistic competence is part of a person's personality, and criticizing someone's style of writing is often like criticizing someone's appearance and looks. People tend to take these things personally and are easily offended. It will therefore require a high degree of diplomacy and tact on the part of the translator to talk to his client or his employer about them.

Furthermore, there are still rather backward opinions in our society about the role of a translator. A translator is often regarded as a linguistic dogsbody. Those who produce the texts in business and industry are usually the ones in positions of power. And translators are usually not. The translator's job still lacks prestige and status. Even those with university degrees are often not regarded as peers by their colleagues who are lawyers, engineers, or executives in the same firm (cf. Stellbrink 1986, passim; Hönig 1992a, passim). What we need is a new understanding of the translator's role and position in industry and commerce and, indeed, in society. Others may be experts in law, engineering and business; translators are experts in languages and cultures and in the production of texts.

Translator-training institutions in many countries have become aware of the importance of producing a new understanding of the translator's task. As far as Europe is concerned, a very good example of this new consciousness is the work of Justa Holz-Mänttäri at Tampere in Finland, but there are many others such as Mona Baker of the Institute of Translation and Interpreting in Great Britain, Roger Bell in London, Daniel Gile in Paris, Basil Hatim and Ian Mason in Edinburgh, Werner Koller in Bergen, Albrecht Neubert in Leipzig, Christiane Nord in Heidelberg, Heidemarie Salevsky in Berlin, Mary Snell-Hornby in Vienna, Hans J. Vermeer in Heidelberg and Wolfram Wilss in Saarbrücken, to name but a few, and there are my colleagues in Germersheim.

Unfortunately, there are translators on the market who lack professional expertise. There are quite a number of translators with no professional training who only have limited, and sometimes very limited, knowledge of foreign languages. There is the secretary who is supposed to know some German or French. There is the colleague who has worked abroad for some time. *Translator*, unfortunately, is an unprotected profession. Anyone can call himself or herself a translator. Those who have had professional training in translation, however, should gradually be able to increase the status of the profession. The training we provide at our translator-training institutions should enable our graduates to fulfil their roles as experts, and the methods presented in this book should help them not only to produce good translations but also to argue as experts. The arguments presented for the evaluation of errors so far and indeed the models and methods described throughout the book can be used when discussing the quality and appropriateness of texts with clients and employers. There is a good chance that once translators behave as experts when talking to other experts they will be regarded as experts in their own right. Let us look at a few examples of text defects in order to illustrate how this arguing could be done.

Sometimes there are obvious factual errors in source texts, such as in the examples quoted by Schmitt (1987:2)

Die 327 m lange Bundesbahn-Neubaustrecke Hannover-Würzburg...gilt als das bedeutendste Bauvorhaben der Bahn seit Gründung der Bundesrepublik Deutschland (VDI 44 (83):10)

Even with only a little geographical knowledge, a translator will realize that 327 meters is too short for the distance between Hannover and Würzburg, and that this measure should read "Kilometer". Similarly in the text

Das Ultraleicht-Flugzeug basiert auf einer mit Segeltuch bespannten Rohrkonstruktion aus Aluminium und wird von einem 500-m^3 Zweitaktmotor angetrieben, der 30 KW leistet (VDI 22 (84).38)

the size of the engine is obviously not 500 m^3 but 500 cm^3. With these factual errors, which are most likely not really errors but misprints, a translator will have no problems in convincing his or her client that the text should here be corrected. In fact, translators can tacitly correct such errors without consulting their clients or the author of the text.

The situation will be more of a problem when there are general communicative defects in a text. I once had to translate a scholarly article which I believed was not particularly well-structured and which I thought ought to be rewritten in some places. So I talked to the editor of the book who in turn consulted the author, but this was done in a very diplomatic way. The author was told, and this was actually true, that for reasons of space his article had to be shortened and that some explanations had to be added and some alterations made in order to adapt it to the readership of the book. The author agreed, and I condensed the article to half its size and changed a few bits here and there. When the author read the translation, he said he was pleased with the results and offered to translate one of my articles into English as a service in return if the need arose. I have not yet had a chance to take up his offer, but it would be interesting to see what he would do with my text.

When teaching source text adaptation, one might consider the kind of role playing mentioned in Chapter 1, section 1.4. The teacher could take on the role of the source text author and the students could play the role of the translator who discusses the correction and improvement of the text with the author. As has been mentioned earlier, we should not only produce good translators but people who can argue as experts and "defend" their translations. Picking up again the topic of our students' psychological attitude discussed in Chapter 1, we should try right from the beginning to build up their self-confidence, and the way this can be done is by providing ways of arguing, which again can be achieved by providing methods of text analysis.

Chapter 7

A summary of strategies

7.1 The rational approach

The proposition about the psychological make-up of a professional translator which is put forward in this book is that self-awareness will breed self-confidence. In translation training self-awareness can be achieved by rational methods. These methods involve a knowledge of comprehension processes (bottom-up and top-down processes, scenes and frames), which, by means of paraphrasing, are closely linked with translation processes. For supplying this knowledge we can draw on psycholinguistic findings and models. With these models at the back of our minds we can then go into further detail by providing methods of text analysis. Two aspects of text analysis have been presented in this book: pragmatic and semantic analysis. In both cases a functional approach has been favoured. Individual text passages have not been seen as isolated units but as having a function within a passage within a text within a situation within a culture.

The functional approach has a great affinity with Skopos theory. The function of a translation is dependent on the knowledge, expectations, values and norms of the target readers, who are again influenced by the situation they are in and by their culture. These factors determine whether the function of the source text or passages in the source text can be preserved or have to be modified or even changed. Very often these decisions have been made by those who commission the translation, which does not always mean they have made the right decisions. Translators in their roles as experts may have to discuss these matters with their clients.

The functional approach together with the psycholinguistic models of comprehension have provided the backcloth for text analysis. In addition, several linguistic models and notions have been used.

On the pragmatic level:

- descriptive stylistics with its model of situational dimensions
- speech-act theory
- the notion of text type and text type conventions

On the semantic level:
- prototypes
- scenes-and-frames
- structural semantics and semantic features
- functional sentence perspective.

I believe that by using these methods at the training stage the translation process with all its various sub-processes - comprehension of the source text, searching for translations, finding translations, deciding which translations to choose from a number that have come to mind and evaluating the final product - will be improved. In addition, at the stage where we search for translations, a knowledge and awareness of creative processes may be very helpful.

All these rationalisations are often very time-consuming. One might argue that in translating one of the most important factors is speed. This is true, but the time invested in these analytical procedures in translator training will be worthwhile. There is a good chance that our students will finally become translators who possess the professional expertise and behaviour they need to take on new responsibilities and fulfil new tasks which add prestige to the profession. As far as speed is concerned, the strategies learnt at the training stage may become internalized and automatized by frequent use, and their application will take less and less time.

7.2 Solving translation problems

In the discussion of the examples in the book a number of techniques and strategies have been mentioned which teachers of translation may wish to recommend to their students when they have to solve translation problems and which I shall list here systematically in the form of instructions.
1. Clarify the function or purpose of your translation. You can discuss a specific translation assignment with those who commission the translation. If you are free to determine the purpose yourself, you will have to analyse the readers' wishes, expectations etc. in order to find the most suitable purpose. Note: even when the overall purpose has been decided on, you will still, when a translation problem turns up, have to think about which function to assign to the problematic text passages.
2. Classify your translation problem. Is it of a pragmatic (situation and style, speech act and illocution, culture, text type conventions) or a semantic (denotative and connotative meaning) nature? Note: One and the same word, phrase, utterance or passage may present different types of problems. Analyse

the problems successively.

3. If the problem is stylistic and situational, run through the situational dimensions presented in section 3.1. and find out which of the dimensions are reflected in the text. Depending on the function of your translation and also on the function of the text passage in question within the overall text, decide which dimensions have to be preserved in the translation. Try to find a translation in which these dimensions are contained. For solution finding you can make use of creative techniques (cf. Chapter 2). Remember there is the parallel-activity technique for removing mental blocks and getting back your fluency of thinking. Remember there is divergent thinking and there are transformations.

4. If there is a problem with the illocution of utterances, classify the illocution by the use of performative verbs. Remember that sometimes there are no performative verbs. You then have to use paraphrases to analyse the function of the speech act. Note: an utterance may express several illocutions at the same time. Find out if the linguistic form of the speech act is stylistically marked, that is, if it is determined by the situation in which it is used. Depending on the function of your translation and also on the function of the speech act within the overall text, decide which illocutions and stylistic features have to be preserved in the translation. Look for a target utterance which contains this illocution (these illocutions) and stylistic features. When doing this try to make use of the creative techniques mentioned in Chapter 2.

5. If the problem is a cultural one, find out if source and target culture coincide or diverge as far as the problem is concerned. If they coincide, there will normally be no cultural problems. However, if the source text does not sufficiently take into account the effect it produces in its own culture, as was the case with Chancellor Kohl's utterance (cf. section 3.3), you may, after functional considerations, consider altering the source text. If source and target culture diverge, you will have to decide, depending on the function of your translation and also on the function of the overall text, if the cultural reference, allusion or implication can be left as it is or has to be explained, dropped, changed or replaced by a target culture equivalent. In your search for solutions, here again remember the creative techniques.

6. If the problem is one of text type conventions, use parallel texts to find out about target text conventions. Note that conventions can be culturally determined (for instance, "closeness" in British academic writing vs. "distance" in German academic texts when the author addresses the reader, cf. section 3.4) Normally source text conventions are replaced by target text conventions, because following conventions helps to achieve smooth communication. For speech acts, such as instructions in leaflets and manuals, regulative rules can be formulated, which can help translators to find

equivalents (cf. section 3.5). Since using conventions means following fixed patterns, creativity does not come into play here.

7. If the problem is one of denotative meaning, "unpack" the meaning of the word or phrase. Use monolingual dictionaries in the comprehension phase. When you interpret the definitions and examples, find out which semantic features are the relevant ones in context. Remember the phenomenon of foregrounding and suppression of semantic features! Depending on the function of your translation and also on the function of the word in question within its context, decide which features have to be preserved in the translation. Remember that you do not have to stick to formal equivalents, but you can use paraphrases, which may be triggered off by the definitions or examples in dictionaries. For solution-finding make use of the creative processes, such as finding synonyms for a given word or phrase or the phenomenon of chaining, that is, joining together notions which are in the same domain of experience.

8. As a complementary method to looking up the meaning of words and phrases in dictionaries, especially when dictionaries provide no clues to their meaning, make use of conscious comprehension processes. Remember that notions, pictures and experiences in your memory which can also be triggered off by the context are the *scenes* which can provide you with the *frames*, that is, they serve as the basis for finding translations. For inferring meaning from context make use of the model of theme and rheme progression as a means of finding out about the line of thought of the text. Depending on the function of your translation and also on the function of the word in question within its context, decide which features of the *scene* have to be preserved in the translation. For solution-finding remember the creative processes mentioned under 7.

9. If the problem is one of connotative or stylistic meaning, infer the meaning of words and phrases from the labels attached to them in dictionaries. If dictionaries do not provide clues or if the clues are too vague, infer the connotative meaning from the context. Make use of situational analysis (cf. no. 3). Depending on the function of your translation and also on the function of the word in question within the overall text, decide which situational dimensions have to be preserved in the translation. Try to find a translation in which these dimensions are contained. Here again, remember the creative techniques listed in 7.

7.3 Evaluating translations

When evaluating our students' translations and grading their errors several steps are involved which are based on the assumption that detecting errors and noticing problems are interrelated. We may assume that when an error occurs there was a problem, although not all problems result in errors. We may have found that when marking a student's translation together with a colleague we will often discuss not only the errors but the problems of the text as such. This is a sign that we cannot grade an error unless we have analysed the problematic text passage. Analysis is the basis for our evaluation. As a result of the examples discussed in Chapter 6 one may take the following steps.

We may begin by classifying the problematic text passage and the resulting errors. This means finding out if a cultural, a situational, an illocutionary, a meaning or a "language" problem is involved (cf. Chapters 2 - 4 on text analysis and Chapter 6 on evaluation and errors). Classifying their problems will be helpful to our students. They will be able to see which areas they have to concentrate on. As their teachers we will be able to find out which areas ought to be dealt with in our teaching. If for instance we find that most students produce errors of word meaning, we may consider spending more time on semantic analysis.

Having classified the problematic passage, we can then analyse its function within its context and with regard to the overall purpose of the translation which we may have specified in the translation task. For this purpose we can make use of the principles of *cohesion* within the text and *coherence* of the text with its function for the readers in a situation and culture.

Grading the error is guided by the question: have the results of our analysis been reproduced in the translation? As we have seen in Chapter 6 evaluation of errors is both a qualitative and a quantitative affair. The errors more difficult to grade are the quantitative (non-binary) ones. The quantitative concept for our grading is expressed by the guiding question: how far-reaching is the error? The *maxim of the necessary degree of precision* proposed in this book for the translator's decision-making can also be used for the grading of all types of errors.

In order to counterbalance our error-based approach we may look for passages in a student's translation which can be evaluated positively. We can do this by observing how the difficult passages which have been revealed to us through other students' errors have been dealt with. Of course, there may be other well-translated passages, but starting off with those which have been a problem for many students at the same stage of training has, in my experience, proved to be a useful basis.

Bibliography

Aitchison, Jean. 1976. *The Articulate Mammal. An Introduction to Psycho-linguistics*. London: Hutchinson of London.

Alexieva, Bistra. 1990."Creativity in simultaneous interpretation". *Babel* 36, no.1.1-6.

Ammann, Margaret. 1989. *Grundlagen der modernen Translationstheorie (th - translatorisches handeln, Band 1)*. Heidelberg 1989.

Arntz, Reiner. 1986. "Terminologievergleich und internationale Termi-nologieangleichung". Snell-Hornby, Mary (ed.). *Übersetzungswissenschaft. Eine Neuorientierung*. Tübingen: Francke. 283-310.

Arntz, Reiner & Picht, Heribert 1989. *Einführung in die Terminologiearbeit*. Hildesheim: Olms (2. Aufl. 1991).

Austin, John L. 1962. *How to do things with words*. Oxford: Clarendon Press.

Baker, Mona. 1992. *In Other Words. A coursebook on Translation*. London and New York: Routledge.

Barclay, J.R., Bransford,John D., Franks, Jeffrey J., McCarrell, Nancy S. & Nitsch, Kathy. 1974. "Comprehension and Semantic Flexibility".*Journal of Verbal Learning and Verbal Behaviour* 13. 471-481.

Baumann, Klaus-Dieter & Kalverkämper, Hartwig, eds.1992. *Kontrastive Fach-sprachenforschung*. Tübingen: Narr.

Bell, Roger. 1991. *Translation and Translating*. London: Longman.

Benson, Morton, Benson, Evelyn & Ilson, Robert. 1986. *The BBI Combinatory Dictionary of English. A Guide to Word Combinations*. Amsterdam/ Philadelphia: Benjamins.

Bergström, R. Matti. 1988. "Communication and Translation from the Point of View of Brain Function". Justa Holz-Mänttäri. ed. *Translationstheorie - Grundlagen und Standorte*. Tampere. 23-38.

156   TRAINING THE TRANSLATOR

Bobrow, Robert J. & Brown, John Seely 1975. "Systematic Understanding: Synthesis, Analysis, and Contingent Knowledge in Specialized Understanding Systems". Bobrow, Daniel G. & Collins, Allan. eds. *Representation and Understanding. Studies in Cognitive Science*. New York: Academic Press. 103-130.

Bühler, Hildegund. 1993. "Vom Wert der Übersetzung und vom Selbstwertgefühl der Übersetzenden". Holz-Mänttäri, Justa & Nord, Christiane. eds. *Traducere Navem. Festschrift für Katharina Reiss zum 70. Geburtstag (studia translatologica* ser. A, vol. 3). Tampere. 91-102.

Catford, J. C. 1965. *A Linguistic Theory of Translation. An Essay in Applied Linguistics*. London: Longman.

Clark, Charles. 1966. *Brainstorming*. Garden City, N.Y.: Doubleday 1958. German translation by B. Wimmer: *Brainstorming*. München: Moderne Industrie.

Clark, Herbert H.& Clark, Eve V. 1977. *Psychology and Language. An Introduction to Psycholinguistics*. New York: Harcourt Brace Jovanovich.

Clyne, Michael. 1981. "Culture and Discourse Structure". *Journal of Pragmatics* 5. 61-66.

Clyne, Michael. 1987. "Cultural differences in the organization of academic texts". *Journal of Pragmatics* 11. 201-238.

Clyne, Michael. 1991. "Zu kulturellen Unterschieden in der Produktion und Wahrnehmung englischer und deutscher wissenschaftlicher Texte". *Info DaF* 18:4. 376-383.

Corder, Pit S. 1973. *Introducing Applied Linguistics*. Harmondsworth: Penguin.

Crystal David & Davy, Derek. 1969. *Investigating English Style*. London: Longman.

Danes, Frantisec. 1978. "Zur linguistischen Analyse der Textstruktur". Dressler, Wolfgang. ed. *Textlinguistik*. Darmstadt: Wissenschafliche Buchgesellschaft. 185-192.

de Bono, Edward. 1970. *Lateral Thinking. A Textbook of creativity*. London: Ward Lock Educational.

Drescher, Horst W. 1987. "Dickens's reputation in Germany. Some remarks on early translations of his novels". J. Albrecht et al. eds.. *Translation und interkulturelle Kommunikation*. Frankfurt am Main: Peter Lang. 307-314.

Engelkamp, Johannes. 1974. *Psycholinguistik*. München: Fink.

Fabricius-Hansen, Cathrine. 1991. "Contrastive Stylistics. Outline of a Research Project on German and Norwegian Non-Fictional Prose". Lauridsen, Karen Marie & Lauridsen, Ole. eds. *Contrastive Linguistics: Papers from the CL-Symposium, 28.-30. August 1989*. The Arhus School of Business. Arhus. 51-75.

Fillmore, Charles J. 1976. "Frame Semantics and the Nature of Language". Harnard, J. et al. eds. *Origins and Evolution of Language and Speech. Annals of the New York Academy of Sciences*. Vol. 280. New York. 20-32.

Fillmore, Charles J. 1977. "Scenes-and-Frames Semantics". Zampolli, Antonio. ed. *Linguistic Structures Processing*. Amsterdam: North Holland. 55-88.

Fillmore, Charles, J. 1977b. "Topics in Lexical Semantics". Cole, Roger W. ed., *Current Issues in Linguistic Theory*. Bloomington and London: Indiana University Press. 76-138.

Fleischmann, Eberhard. 1991. "Zur Rolle der Verbalisierungen bei professionellen Übersetzern". Schmitt, Christian. ed. *Neue Methoden der Sprachmittlung*. Wilhelmsfeld: Egert. 13-20.

Galtung, Johan. 1985. "Struktur, Kultur und intellektueller Stil. Ein vergleichender Essay über sachsonische, teutonische, gallische und nipponische Wissenschaft". Wierlacher, Alois. ed. *Das Fremde und das Eigene: Prolegomena zu einer interkulturellen Germanistik*. München: Iudicium Verlag.151-193.

Gerloff, Pamela. 1988. From French to English: A Look at the Translation Process in Students, Bilinguals, and Professionals. Mimeo. Harvard University unpublished dissertation.

Gerzymisch-Arbogast, Heidrun. 1986. "Zur Relevanz der Thema-Rhema-Gliederung für den Übersetzungsprozeß". Snell-Hornby, Mary. ed. *Übersetzungswissenschaft - eine Neuorientierung*. Tübingen: Francke. 160-183.

Getzels, J.W. 1975. "Creativity: Prospects and Issues". Taylor, Irving A. & Getzels, J.W. eds. *Perspectives in Creativity*. Chicago: Aldine. 326-344.

Gläser, Rosemarie. 1990. *Fachtextsorten im Englischen (=Forum für Fachsprachenforschung Band 13). Tübingen: Narr.*

Gläser, Rosemarie.1992. "Methodische Konzepte für das Tertium comparationis in der Fachsprachenforschung - dargestellt an anglistischen und nordistschen Arbeiten". Baumann, Klaus-Dieter & Kalverkämper, Hartwig eds. *Kontrastive Fachsprachenforschung.* Tübingen: Narr. 78-92.

Göpferich, Susanne. 1993. "Die translatorische Behandlung von Textsorten-konventionen in technischen Texten". *Lebende Sprachen* 28/2. 49-53.

Greenbaum, Sidney. 1969. *Studies in English Adverbial Usage.* London: Longman.

Grice, H. Paul. 1975. "Logic and conversation". Cole, P.& Morgan, J.L. eds. *Syntax and Semantics. Vol.3: Speech Acts.* New York: Academic Press. 41-58.

Guilford, Joy Peter. 1959. *Personality.* New York: McGraw-Hill. German Translation: *Persönlichkeit. Logik, Methodik und Ergebnisse ihrer quantitativen Erforschung.* Übertragen von Heinrich Kottenhoff und Ursula Agrell. Weinheim und Basel: Beltz 1964.

Guilford, Joy Peter. 1975. "Creativity: A Quarter Century of Progress". Taylor, I.A. & Getzels, J.W. eds. *Perspectives in Creativity.* Chicago: Aldine. 37-59.

Gutt, Ernst-August. 1990. "A Theoretical Account of Translation - Without a Translation Theory". *Target* 2:2. 135-164.

Gutt, Ernst-August. 1991. *Translation and Relevance. Cognition and Context.* Oxford: Blackwell.

Halliday, M.A.K. & Hasan, Ruqaiya. 1976. *Cohesion in English.* London: Longman.

Halliday, M.A.K., McIntosh, Angus & Strevens, Peter. 1964. *The Linguistic Sciences and Laguage Teaching.* London: Longman.

Handwerker, Brigitte. 1988. "Wortbedeutung und Textverstehen". Arntz, Reiner. ed. *Textlinguistik und Fachsprache.* Hildesheim: Olms. 333-347.

Hatim, Basil & Mason, Ian. 1990. *Discourse and the Translator.* London: Longman.

Holz-Mänttäri, Justa. 1986. "Translatorisches Handeln - theoretisch fundierte Berufsprofile". Snell-Hornby, Mary. ed. *Übersetzungswissenschaft. Eine Neuorientierung.* Tübingen: Francke 1986. 348-374.

Holz-Mänttäri, Justa. 1984. *Translatorisches Handeln. Theorie und Methode.* Helsinki: Annales Academicae Scientiarum Fennicae.

Holz-Mänttäri, Justa & Nord, Christiane, eds. 1993. *Traducere Navem. Festschrift für Katharina Reiss zum 70. Geburtstag (=studia translatologica ser. A, vol. 3).*Tampere.

Hönig, Hans G. 1986. Übersetzen zwischen Reflex und Reflexion - Ein Modell der übersetzungsrelevanten Textanalyse". Snell-Hornby, Mary. ed.. *Übersetzungswissenschaft. Eine Neuorientierung.* Tübingen: Francke. 230-251.

Hönig, Hans G. 1987. "Wer macht die Fehler?" Albrecht, Jörn et al. eds. *Translation und interkulturelle Kommunikation.* Frankfurt am Main: Peter Lang. 37-46.

Hönig, Hans G. 1988a. "Übersetzen lernt man nicht durch Übersetzen". *Fremdsprachen lehren und lernen. FLuL.* 17.Jg.1988. 154-167.

Hönig, Hans G. 1988b. "Wissen Übersetzer eigentlich, was sie tun?" *Lebende Sprachen* 1/1988. 10-14.

Hönig, Hans G. 1990. "Sagen, was man nicht weiß - wissen was man nicht sagt. Überlegungen zur übersetzerischen Intuition". Arntz, Reiner & Thome, Gisela, eds. *Übersetzungswissenschaft. Ergebnisse und Perspektiven. Festschrift für Wolfram Wilss zum 65.Geburtstag.* Tübingen: Narr. 152-161.

Hönig, Hans G. 1991. "Holmes' 'Mapping Theory' and the Landscape of Mental Translation Processes". Van Leuven-Zwart, Kitty & Naaijkens, Ton, eds. *Translation Studies: The State of the Art. Proceedings of the First James S Holmes Symposium on Translation Studies.* Amsterdam: Rodopi. 91-101.

Hönig, Hans G. 1992. "Von der erzwungenen Selbstentfremdung des Übersetzers - ein offener Brief an Justa Holz-Mänttäri". *TextConText* 7, 1/1992. 1-14.

Hönig, Hans G. 1993. "Vom Selbst-Bewußtsein des Übersetzers". Holz-Mänttäri, Justa & Nord, Christiane, eds. *Traducere Navem. Festschrift für Katharina Reiss zum 70. Geburtstag (=studia translatologica ser. A, vol. 3).*

Hönig, Hans G. & Kussmaul, Paul. 1982. *Strategie der Übersetzung. Ein Lehr- und Arbeitsbuch.* Tübingen: Narr.

Hörmann, Hans. 1976. *Meinen und Verstehen. Grundzüge einer psychologischen Semantik.* Frankfurt am Main: Suhrkamp.

Hörmann, Hans. 1981. *Einführung in die Psycholinguistik.* Darmstadt: Wiss. Buchgesellschaft.

House, Juliane. 1977. *A Model for Translation Quality Assessment.* Tübingen: Narr 1977.

House, Juliane. 1988. "Talking to oneself or thinking with others". in: *Fremd sprachen Lehren und Lernen, FLuL 1988.* 84-98.

House, Juliane & Blum-Kulka, Shoshana, eds.1986. *Interlingual and Intercultural Communication.* Tübingen: Narr.

Jääskeläinen, Riitta. 1989. "Translation Assignment in Professional vs. Nonprofessional Translation: A Think-Aloud Protocol Study". Séguinot, Candace. ed. *The Translation Process.* Toronto: H.G. Publications, School of Translation, York University. 87-98.

Jääskeläinen, Riitta. 1993. "Investigating Translation Strategies". Tirkkonen-Condit & Laffling, John. eds. *Recent Trends in Empirical Translation Research (=Studies in Languages. University of Joensuu, Faculty of Arts No. 28).* Joensuu.

Katz, J.& Fodor, J. 1963. "The structure of a semantic theory". *Language* 39, 1963. 170-210.

Kiraly, Donald Charles. 1990. Toward a systematic approach to translation skills instruction. Ann Arbor: U.M.I.

Koller, Werner. 1979. *Einführung in die Übersetzungswissenschaft,* Heidelberg: Quelle und Meyer.

Königs, Frank G. 1979. *Übersetzung in Theorie und Praxis. Ansatzpunkte für die Konzeption einer Didaktik der Übersetzung.* Bochum: Seminar für Sprachlehrforschung.

Königs, Frank G. 1987. "Was beim Übersetzen passiert: Theoretische Aspekte, empirische Befunde und praktische Konsequenzen". *Die Neueren Sprachen* 86/2.193-215.

Königs, Frank G. 1991. "Dem Übersetzen den Prozess machen?" Psycholinguistische Überlegungen zum Übersetzen und ihre didaktischen Konsequezen". Iwasaki, Eijiro. ed. *Begegnung mit dem "Fremden". Grenzen - Traditionen - Vergleiche. Akten des VIII. Internationalen Germanisten-Kongresses Tokyo 1990*, Band 5. München: Iudicium Verlag. 132-141.

Krings, Hans-Peter. 1986a. *Was in den Köpfen von Übersetzern vorgeht: Eine empirische Untersuchung zur Struktur des Übersetzungsprozesses an fortgeschrittenen Französischlernern.* Tübingen: Narr.

Krings, Hans. 1986b. "Translation Problems and Translation Strategies of Advanced German Learners of French (L2)". House, Juliane & Blum-Kulka, Shoshana, eds. *Interlingual and Intercultural Communication.* Tübingen: Narr. 263-276.

Krings, Hans P. 1987. "Der Übersetzungsprozeß bei Berufsübersetzern - Eine Fallstudie". Arntz, R. ed. *Textlinguistik und Fachsprache. Akten des Internationalen übersetzungswissenschaftlichen AILA-Symposiums Hildesheim 13.-16.4.1987.* Hildesheim: Olms.

Kupsch-Losereit, Sigrid. 1986. "Scheint eine schöne Sonne? oder: Was ist ein Übersetzungsfehler?" *Lebende Sprachen* 1/1986. 12-16.

Kupsch-Losereit, Sigrid. 1988. "Die Übersetzung als soziale Praxis". *Fremdsprachen lehren und lernen, FLuL.* 17. 28-40.

Kupsch-Losereit, S. & Kussmaul, P. 1982. "Stilistik und Übersetzen". *Lebende Sprachen* 3/1982. 101-104.

Kussmaul, Paul. 1974. *Bertolt Brecht und das englische Drama der Renaissance.* Bern und Frankfurt am Main: Herbert Lang.

Kussmaul, Paul. 1977. "Englische Modalverben und Sprechakte". *Neusprachliche Mitteilungen* 4/1977. 202 - 207.

Kussmaul, Paul. 1978a. "Kommunikationskonventionen in Textsorten am Beispiel deutscher und englischer geisteswissenschaftlicher Abhandlungen". *Lebende Sprachen* 2/1978. 54-58.

Kussmaul, Paul. 1978b. "In fact, actually, anyway...: Indikatoren von Sprechakten im informellen gesprochenen Englisch". *Die Neueren Sprachen* 3/4, 1978. 357 - 369.

Kussmaul, Paul. 1980.ed. *Sprechakttheorie. Ein Reader*. Wiesbaden: Athenaion.

Kussmaul, Paul.1985. "The Degree of Semantic Precision in Translation". *Babel,* Vol. XXXI, No.1. 12-19.

Kussmaul, Paul. 1986. "Übersetzen als Entscheidungsprozess. Die Rolle der Fehleranalyse in der Übersetzungsdidaktik" Snell-Hornby, Mary. ed. *Übersetzungswissenschaft. Eine Neuorientierung*. Tübingen 1986. 206-229.

Kussmaul, Paul. 1987. "Pragmatik und Übersetzungstheorie". Ehnert, R. & Schleyer, W. eds. *Übersetzen im Fremdsprachenunterricht. Beiträge zur Übersetzungswissenschaft - Annäherungen an eine Übersetzungsdidaktik (= Materialien Deutsch als Fremdsprache Bd. 26)*. Regensburg. 25-32.

Kussmaul, Paul. 1987b. "Übersetzen - aber nicht ins Blaue hinein". Jörn Albrecht et al. eds. *Translation und interkulturelle Kommunikation*. Frankfurt am Main: Peter Lang. 27-36.

Kussmaul, Paul. 1988. "Ein neuer Vorschlag: die Herübersetzung gehört in den Deutschunterricht". *Der Deutschunterricht* 4/1988. 83-89.

Kussmaul, Paul. 1989a. "Toward an empirical Investigation of the translation process: Translating a passage from S.I. Hayakawa. *Symbol, Status and Personality"*. von Bardeleben, Renate. ed. *Wege amerikanischer Kultur. Ways and Byways of American Culture. Aufsätze zu Ehren von Gustav H. Blanke*. Frankfurt am Main: Lang. 369-380.

Kussmaul, Paul. 1989b. "Interferenzen im Übersetzungsprozess - Diagnose und Therapie". Schmidt, Heide ed. *Interferenz in der Translation*. Leipzig: Enzyklopädie. 19-28.

Kussmaul, Paul. 1990. "Die Übersetzung von Sprechakten in Textsorten". *Der Deutschunterricht* , Jg.42, Heft 1.17-22.

Kussmaul, Paul. 1991. "Creativity in the Translation Process. Empirical Approaches". Van Leuven-Zwart, Kitty & Naaijkens, Ton. eds. *Translation Studies: The State of the Art. Proceedings of the First James S Holmes Symposium on Translation Studies*. Amsterdam: Rodopi. 91-101.

Kvam, Sigmund. 1985. "Partizipialkonstruktionen und Partizipialattribute in deutschen Fachtexten der Wirtschaft" von Polenz, Peter, Johannes Erben & Goossens, Jan. eds. *Sprachnormen: lösbare und unlösbare Probleme/ Kontroversen um die neuere deutsche Sprachgeschichte/ Dialektologie und Soziolinguistik: Die Kontroverse um die Mundartforschung (=Kontroversen, alte und neue. Akten des VII. Internationalen Germanisten-Kongresses Göttingen 1985*, Band 4). 105-119.

Kvam, Sigmund. 1992. "Zur Rolle von Paralleltexten bei der Translation - Am Beispiel deutsch-norwegischer Übersetzungsfälle". *TextconText* 7: 3 und 4. 193-217.

Lakoff, George. 1987. *Women, Fire and Dangerous Things. What Categories Reveal about the Mind*. Chicago: University of Chicago Press.

Landau, Erika. 1969. *Psychologie der Kreativität*. München: Reinhardt.

Larson, Mildred L. 1984. *Meaning-based Translation*. Boston: University Press of America.

Leech, Geoffrey. 1974. *Semantics*. Harmondsworth: Penguin Books.

Leisi, Ernst. 1973. *Praxis der englischen Semantik*. Heidelberg: Winter.

Lörscher, Wolfgang. 1986. "Linguistic Aspects of Translation Processes: Toward an Analysis of Translation Performance". House, Juliane & Blum-Kulka, Shoshana, eds. *Interlingual and Intercultural Communication*. Tübingen: Narr. 277-292.

Lörscher, Wolfgang. 1991. *Translation Performance, Translation Process, and Translation Strategies. A Psycholinguistic Investigation*. Tübingen: Narr.

Lörscher, Wolfgang. 1992a. "Process-oriented research into translation and implications for translation teaching". *Traduction, Terminologie, Rédaction (TTR)*, Vol.5, no.1, 1992. 145-161.

Lörscher, Wolfgang.1992b. "Translation Process Analysis". *Proceedings of the Fourth Scandinavian Symposium on Translation Theory,* June 4-6, 1992, University of Turku (forthcoming).

Lundquist, James.1979. *J.D. Salinger*. New York: Frederick Unger.

Mel'cuk, I.A., Arbatschevsky-Jumarie, N., Elnitsky, L., Iordanskaya, L.& Lessard, A. eds. 1984. *Dictionnaire explicatif et combinatoire du francais contemporain*. Montreal: Les Presses de L'Université de Montréal.

Mel'cuk, I.A. & Zolkovsky, A.K. 1984. *Explanatory Combinatorial Dictionary of Modern Russian: Semantico-Syntactic Studies of Russian Vocabulary*. (=*Wiener Slawistischer Almanach, Sonderband 14*) Wien.

Neubert, Albrecht. 1984."Text-bound Translation Teaching". Wilss, Wolfram & Thome, Gisela, eds. *Die Theorie des Übersetzens und ihr Aufschlußwert für die Übersetzungs- und Dolmetschdidaktik. Translation Theory ad its Implementation in the Teaching of Translating and Interpreting*. Tübingen: Narr. 61-70.

Neubert, Albrecht. 1988. "Top-down-Prozeduren beim translatorischen Informationstransfer". Jäger, Gert & Neubert, Albrecht, eds. *Semantik, Kognition und Äquivalenz*. Leipzig: VEB Verlag Enzyklopädie.18-30.

Neubert, Albrecht & Shreve, Gregory M. 1992. *Translation as Text*. Kent, Ohio: The Kent State University Press.

Newmark, Peter. 1981. *Approaches to Translation*. Oxford: Pergamon.

Nida, Eugene A. 1964a. *Toward a Science of Translating. With Special Reference to Principles and Procedures Involved in Bible Translating*. Leiden: Brill.

Nida, Eugene A. 1964b. "Linguistics and Ethnology". Hymes, Dell. ed. *Language in Culture and Society. A Reader in Linguistics and Anthropology*. New York: Harper and Row. 90-100.

Nida, Eugene A. 1974. "Semantic structure and translating". Wilss, Wolfram & Thome, Gisela, eds. *Aspekte der theoretischen, sprachenpaarbezogenen und angewandten Übersetzungswissenschaft II*. Heidelberg: Groos. 33-63 .

Nida, Eugene A. 1975. *Componential Analysis of Meaning. An Introduction to Semantic Structures*. Den Haag/Paris: Brill.

Nida, Eugene A. & Taber, Charles. 1969. *The Theory and Practice of Translation*. Leiden: Brill.

Nord, Christiane. 1988. *Textanalyse und Übersetzen*. Heidelberg: Groos. (English version: *Text analysis in Translation*. Amsterdam: Rodopi 1991)

Nord, Christiane. 1992. "Text analysis in translator training". Dollerup, Cay & Loddegaard, Anne, eds. *Teaching translation and Interpreting. Training, Talent and Experience*. Amsterdam/Philadelphia: Benjamins. 39-48.

Osborn, A.F. 1953. *Applied imagination: Principles and procedures of creative thinking*. New York: Scribner's.

Preiser, Siegfried. 1976. *Kreativitätsforschung*. Darmstadt: Wissenschaftliche Buchgesellschaft.

Pym, Anthony. 1992. "Translation error analysis and the interface with language teaching" Dollerup, Cay & Loddegaard, Anne. eds. *Teaching translation and Interpreting. Training, Talent and Experience*. Amsterdam/Philadelphia: Benjamins. 279-290.

Reiss, Katharina. 1971. *Möglichkeiten und Grenzen der Übersetzungskritik*. München: Hueber.

Reiss, Katharina. 1976. *Texttyp und Übersetzungsmethode. Der operative Text*. Kronberg im Taunus: Scriptor.

Reiss, Katharina & Vermeer, Hans J. 1984. *Grundlegung einer allgemeinen Translationstheorie*. Tübingen: Niemeyer.

Rosch, Eleanor. 1973. "Natural categories". *Cognitive Psychology* 4. 1973. 328-350.

Sager, Juan C. 1983. "Quality annd standards - the evaluation of translations". Picken, Catriona. ed. *The Translator's Handbook*. London: Aslib. 121-128.

Sager, Juan C. 1993. *Language Engineering and Translation. Consequences of Automation*. Amsterdam: Benjamins.

Séguinot, Candace. ed. 1989. *The Translation Process*. Toronto: H.G. Publications. School of Translation. York University.

Schmitt, Peter A. 1985. "Interkulturelle Kommunikationsprobleme in multinationalen Konzernen". *Lebende Sprachen* 1/1985. 1-9.

Schmitt, Peter A. 1986. "Die 'Eindeutigkeit' von Fachtexten: Bemerkungen zu einer Fiktion". Snell-Hornby, Mary ed. *Übersetzungswissenschaft. Eine Neuorientierung*. Tübingen: Francke 1986. 252-282.

Schmitt, Peter A. 1987. "Fachtextübersetzung und 'Texttreue': Bemerkung zur Qualität von Ausgangstexten". *Lebende Sprachen*, 23. Jg., 1/1987. 1-7.

Schmitt, Peter A. 1992. "Culturally specific elements in technical translation". Schwend, Joachim, Hagemann, Susanne & Völkel, Hermann, eds. *Literatur im Kontext - Literature in Context. Festschrift für Horst W. Drescher.* Frankfurt am Main: Peter Lang. 495-515.

Schröder, Hartmut. 1987a. "Hedging and its linguistic realizations in German, English, and Finnish philosophical texts: a case study". *Erikoiskielet ja käännösteoria. VAKKI-seminaari VII.* Vaasa 1987. 47-57.

Schröder, Hartmut. 1987. "Kontrastive Textanalysen - Ein Projekt zur Erforschung des Zusammenhangs von Diskurs, Kultur, Paradigma und Sprache in argumentativen Fachtexten der Gesellschaftswissenschaften". *Finlance - The Finnnish Journal of Language and Language Teaching,* Vol. VI. 145-173.

Schröder, Konrad & Finkenstaedt, Thomas, eds. 1977. *Reallexikon der englischen Fachdidaktik.* Darmstadt: Wissenschaftliche Buchgesellschaft.

Searle, John R. 1969. *Speech Acts. An Essay in the Philosophy of Language.* Cambridge: Cambridge University Press.

Searle, John R. 1972. "What is a Speech Act?". Giglioli, P.P. ed. *Language and social context.* Harmondsworth: Penguin Books. 136 - 154.

Searle, John R. 1975. "Indirect Speech Acts". Cole, P. & Morgan, J.L. eds. *Syntax and Semantics. Vol.3: Speech Acts.* New York: Academic Press. 59-82.

Searle, John R. 1976. "A classification of illocutionary acts". *Language in Society* 5.1-23.

Selekovitch, Danica.1976. "Interpretation. A Psychological Approach to Translating". Brislin, R.W. ed. *Translation. Applications and Research.* New York: Gardner. 92-115.

Smith, Veronica & Klein-Braley, Christine. 1985. *In Other Words. Arbeitsbuch Übersetzung.* München: Hueber.

Snell-Hornby, Mary. ed. 1986. *Übersetzungswissenschaft. Eine Neuorientierung.* Tübingen: Francke.

Snell-Hornby, Mary. 1988. *Translation Studies. An Integrated Approach.* Amsterdam: Benjamins.

Snell-Hornby, Mary, Pöchhacker, Franz & Kaindl, Klaus, eds. 1994. *Translation Studies. An Interdiscipline. Selected papers from the conference, Vienna, September 1992.* Amsterdam: Benjamins.

Stanley-Jones, D. 1970. *Kybernetics of Mind and Brain.* Springfield/Illinois: Charles C. Thomas.

Stein, Dieter. 1980. "Korrespondenz in kontrastiver Lexik". *Linguistik und Didaktik* 42. 160-167.

Steiner, George. 1975. *After Babel. Aspects of Language and Translation.* London: Oxford University Press.

Stellbrink, Hans-Jürgen. 1986. "Effizienz, Produktivität, Leistung und Status in einem Fremdsprachendienst der Industrie". *Mitteilungsblatt für Dolmetscher und Übersetzer,* 1/1986. 4-5.

Stolze, Radegundis. 1992. *Hermeneutisches Übersetzen. Linguistische Kategorien des Verstehens und Formulierens beim Übersetzen.* Tübingen: Narr.

Tannen, Deborah. 1979. "What's in a Frame? Surface evidence for underlying expectations". Fredle, R.B. ed. *New directions in discourse processing.* Norwood, N.S: Ablex. 137-182.

Tannen, Deborah. 1991. *Du kannst mich einfach nicht verstehen. Warum Männer und Frauen aneinander vorbeireden.* Gütersloh: Bertelsman. (Translation of *You just don't understand. Women and Men in Conversation.* New York: William Morrow)

Taylor, Insup. 1976. *Introduction to Psycholinguistics.* New York: Holt, Rinehart and Winston.

Taylor, Irving A.1975. "A Retrospective View of Creativity Investigation". Taylor, I.A. & Getzels, J.W. eds. *Perspectives in Creativity.* Chicago: Aldine. 1-34.

Tirkkonen-Condit, Sonja. 1989. "Professional vs. Non-Professional Translation: A Think-Aloud Protocol Study" Séguinot, Candace. ed. *The Translation Process.* Toronto: H.G. Publications, School of Translation. York University. 73-85.

Tirkkonen-Condit, Sonja. 1992. "The Interaction of World Knowledge and Linguistic Knowledge in the Process of Translation. A Think-Aloud Protocol Study". Lewandowska-Tomaszczyk, Barbara & Thelen, Marcel, eds. *Translation and Meaning. Proceedings of the Lodz Session of the 1990 Maastricht-Lodz Duo Colloquium on "Translation and Meaning", held in Lodz, Poland, 20-22 September 1990*. Maastricht: Faculty of Translation and Interpreting. 433-440.

Toury, Gideon. 1991. "Experimentation in Translation Studies: Achievements, Prospects and Some Pitfalls". Tirkkonen-Condit, Sonja. ed. *Empirical research in Translation and Intercultural Studies*. Tübingen: Narr. 45 - 66.

Ulmann, Gisela. 1968. *Kreativität. Neue amerikanische Ansätze zur Erweiterung des Intelligenzkonzepts*. Weinheim: Beltz.

van der Wouden, Ton. 1992. "Prolegomena to a multilingual description of collocations". Tommola, Hannu, Varantola, Krista, Salmi-Tolonen, Tarja & Schopp, Jürgen, eds. *Euralex'92 Proceedings I-II, Part I. (=studia translatologica. ser. A, vol. 2)* Tampere. 449-456.

Van Leuven-Zwart, Kitty & Naaijkens, Ton, eds. 1991. *Translation Studies: The State of the Art. Proceedings of the First James S Holmes Symposium on Translation Studies*. Amsterdam: Rodopi.

Vannerem, Mia & Snell-Hornby, Mary. 1986. "Die Szene hinter dem Text: "scenes-and-frames semantics" in der Übersetzung". Mary Snell-Hornby. ed. *Übersetzungswissenschaft - eine Neuorientierung*. Tübingen: Francke 1986. 184-205.

Vermeer, Hans J. 1978. "Ein Rahmen für eine allgemeine Translationstheorie". *Lebende Sprachen* 1978/3. 99-102.

Vermeer, Hans J. 1986. "Übersetzen als kultureller Transfer". Snell-Hornby, Mary. ed. *Übersetzungswissenschaft - eine Neuorientierung*. Tübingen: Francke 1986. 30-53.

Vermeer, Hans J. 1989. *Skopos und Translationsauftrag. (= th - translatorisches handeln, Band 2)* Heidelberg.

Vermeer, Hans J. & Witte, Heidrun. 1990. *Mögen Sie Zistrosen? Scenes & frames & channels im translatorischen Handeln*. Heidelberg: Groos.

Vinay, J.P. & Darbelnet, J. 1968. *Stylistique comparée du francais et de l'anglais. Méthode de traduction.* Paris: Didier 4. Aufl.

Wilss, Wolfram. 1977. *Übersetzungswissenschaft. Probleme und Methoden.* Stuttgart: Klett.

Wilss, Wolfram. 1982. *The Science of Translation.* Tübingen: Narr.

Wilss, Wolfram. 1988. *Kognition und Übersetzen. Zur Theorie und Praxis der menschlichen und der maschinellen Übersetzung.* Tübingen: Niemeyer.

Wilss, Wolfram. 1989. *Zur Manifestation von Kreativität und Routine in der Sprachverwendung.* Tübingen: Niemeyer.

Wilss, Wolfram. 1993. "Projekt übersetzungsdidaktische Grundlagenforschung". *Lebende Sprachen* XXVIII/2. 53-54.

Subject Index

Author Index